modern
crochet
style

15 colourful crochet patterns for you and your home, including fun sustainable makes

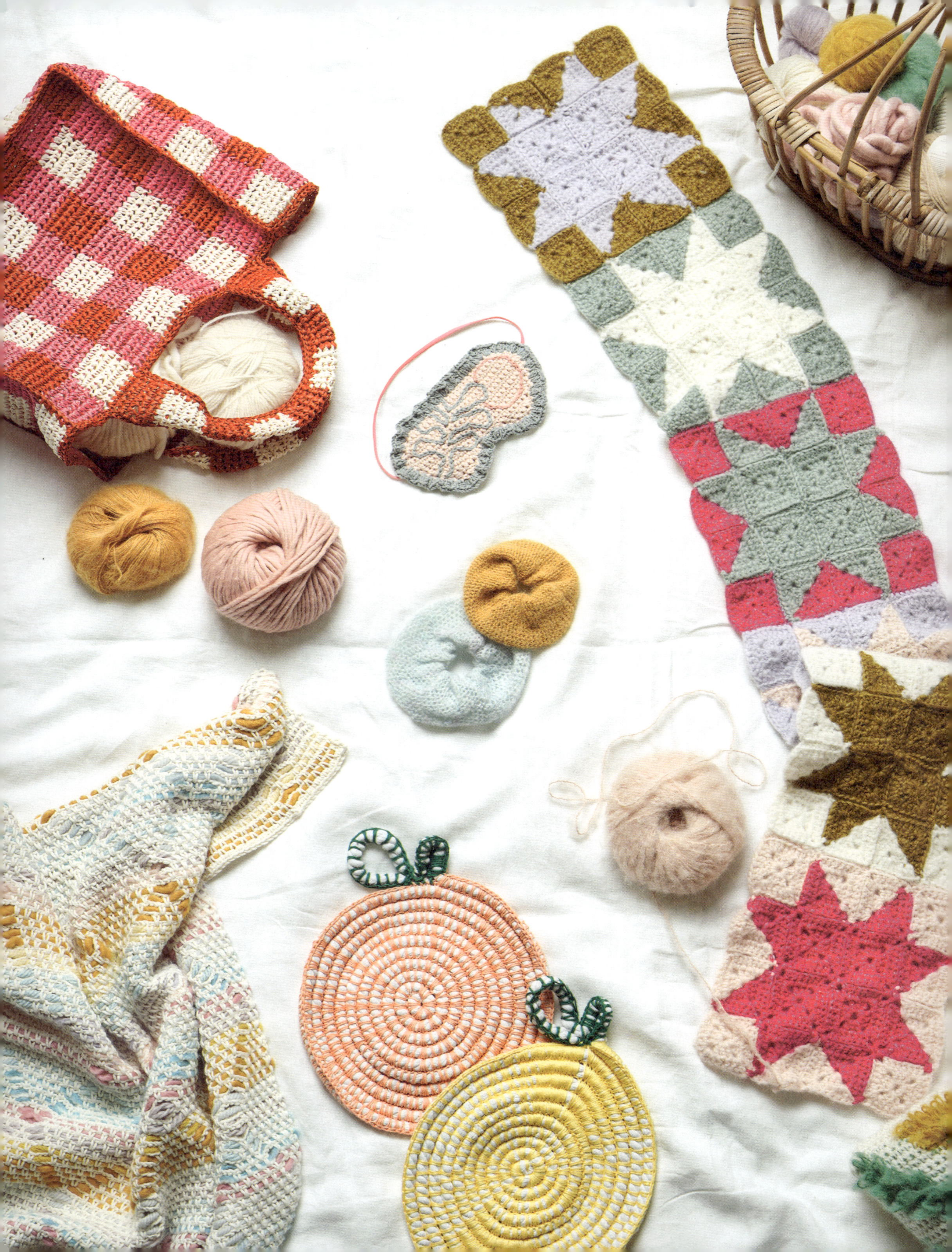

modern
crochet
style

15 colourful crochet patterns for you and your
home, including fun sustainable makes

LINDSEY NEWNS

Photographs by Jesse Wild & Lindsey Newns

White Owl

To all my friends, online and offline, and my family for their support during this making of this book, but especially to my mum and dad for always encouraging my creativity.

First published in Great Britain in 2021 by
PEN & SWORD WHITE OWL
An imprint of Pen & Sword Books Ltd
Yorkshire – Philadelphia

Copyright © Lindsey Newns, 2021
@lottieandalbert

ISBN 9781526793133

The right of Lindsey Newns to be identified as Author of this work has been asserted by her in accordance with the Copyright, Designs and Patents Act 1988.

A CIP catalogue record for this book is available from the British Library.

All rights reserved. No part of this book may be reproduced or transmitted in any form or by any means, electronic or mechanical including photocopying, recording or by any information storage and retrieval system, without permission from the Publisher in writing.

Group Publisher: Jonathan Wright
Series Editor and Publishing Consultant: Katherine Raderecht
Art Director: Jane Toft
Editor: Katherine Raderecht
Photography: Jessie Wild
Styling: Jaine Bevan

Printed and bound in India by Replika Press Pvt. Ltd.

Pen & Sword Books Ltd incorporates the Imprints of Pen & Sword Books
Pen & Sword Books Limited incorporates the imprints of Atlas, Archaeology, Aviation, Discovery, Family History, Fiction, History, Maritime, Military, Military Classics, Politics, Select, Transport, True Crime, Air World, Frontline Publishing, Leo Cooper, Remember When, Seaforth Publishing, The Praetorian Press, Wharncliffe Local History, Wharncliffe Transport, Wharncliffe True Crime and White Owl.

For a complete list of Pen & Sword titles please contact:
PEN & SWORD BOOKS LIMITED
47 Church Street, Barnsley, South Yorkshire S70 2AS, England
E-mail: enquiries@pen-and-sword.co.uk
Website: www.pen-and-sword.co.uk
or
PEN AND SWORD BOOKS
1950 Lawrence Rd, Havertown, PA 19083, USA
E-mail: Uspen-and-sword@casematepublishers.com
Website: www.penandswordbooks.com

contents

Introduction 06
How to Use This Book 08
Abbreviations & Conversions 10
Techniques 12

CHAPTER ONE: SPRING
1. Luxe Scrunchies 24
2. Gingham Bag 28
3. Woven Wallhanging 34
4. Textured Cloths 40

CHAPTER TWO: SUMMER
5. Matisse Eye Mask 46
6. Loopy Cushion 50
7. Tassel Basket 56
8. Fruit Placemats 60

CHAPTER THREE: AUTUMN
9. Slogan Bathmat 66
10. Pom Pom Duffel Bag 72
11. Patchwork Scarf 78

CHAPTER FOUR: WINTER
12. Geo Hat 84
13. Leopard Cowl 90
14. Scrap Rug 96
15. Scandi Stocking 102

FAQs 108
Suppliers 110
About the Author 112

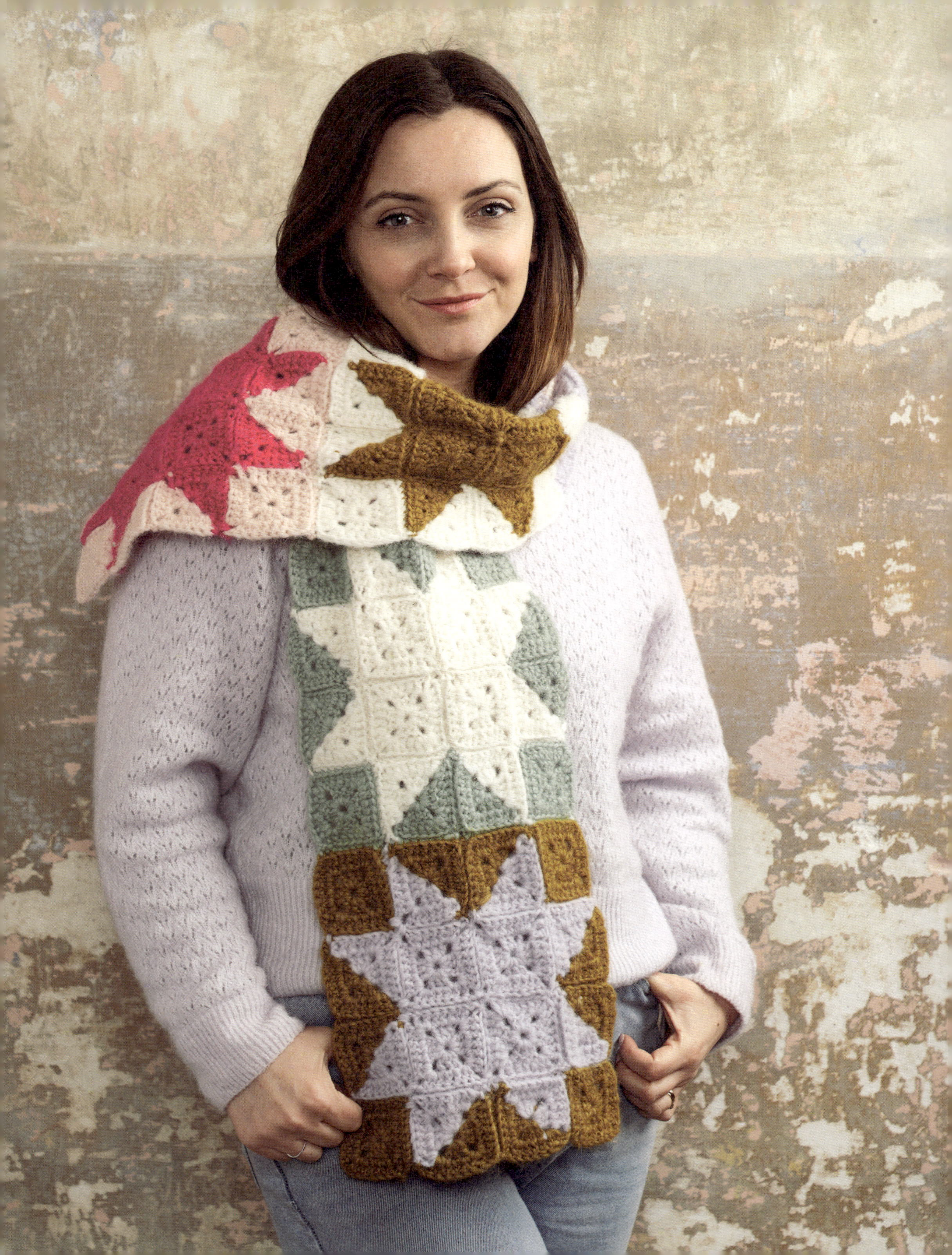

introduction

Accessories are my favourite things to crochet. If you're looking for something that's a bit quicker to make than crochet blankets or garments, then this is the book for you! Here you will find seasonal projects for you and your home, including a real a mix of my favourite yarns, techniques, and crochet styles.

I started to crochet with the infamous granny square, as I'm sure many of you did too, but I soon learned there was so much more to this yarn craft - from tapestry crochet and filet crochet, to working in the round and making 3D baskets and bags. Although this book doesn't contain every crochet technique, you will learn something different with each project. Longer bag and rug projects sit alongside quick evening makes, and simple baskets nestle amongst more complex tapestry-crochet cushions.

When choosing yarns, I wanted to showcase a real variety of fibres. We all know that acrylic is great for washable garments, and that wool is wonderfully warm, but what about raffia yarn? Or hemp or 10mm cotton cord? Or a gorgeously chunky Merino yarn? If you haven't experimented with yarns, then I hope some of the projects in this book will tempt you to be more adventurous. There is a little yarn profile on each project page where I share details of the fibre properties in each make. I was determined to include a couple of scrap yarns projects in this book - and some more sustainable yarns too. Using up scraps is both satisfying and a good way to be more mindful of the environment.

I've enjoyed creating the projects in this book over a year. The bath mat and gingham bag were crocheted in the spring, while my children played in the garden. The pom pom bag and loopy cushion came on holiday with us in the summer, and the patchwork scarf took me through the Christmas holidays.

One of the reasons I took up crochet (after a childhood full of sticking, sewing and making) was because as soon as I picked up a hook, I immediately realised how easy it was to fit in five minutes of crochet here and there. In between making snacks for small folk, or before going to work, or in the evening to relax: no large equipment to get out; no fear of stitches unravelling or sharp needles lost down the side of a sofa. A hook and a ball of yarn can go anywhere with you (in fact I highly recommend always carrying a project with you). I hope this book encourages you to try a new technique or a new yarn but, more importantly, that is sparks joy, and that the moments you spend creating the projects from these pages are happy ones. Happy crocheting! Lindsey x

how to use this book

The book is laid out project-by-project, with all the abbreviations listed in the Abbreviations section at the beginning of the book. I have also included a Techniques section, which details any unusual techniques and stitch descriptions for stitches used in the book. If you are new to crochet, these sections will help you to get better acquainted with the different techniques. If you are more of a seasoned crocheter, feel free to dive straight in at the project pages. Any unusual techniques and special stitches are also listed under the heading 'Techniques' at the start of each project, so you can easily see the information that will be useful to you when starting your make.

The charts included in the book all read slightly differently, depending on the style of crochet used in the project. I have given a detailed explanation on the individual project pages.

The yarns I have listed in each project will work well for the pattern, and have been chosen because I love them. However, I'm also keen you should be able to use your stash and substitute your own chosen yarn where possible, particularly if you want to look at animal-free or plastic free-alternatives. To help you do this, I have listed the weight of the yarn, as well as a detailed breakdown of the fibre, and the meterage/yardage required, so you can substitute your own yarn easily.

If you are substituting yarns, these are the main things you will want to match up: fibre, yardage and weight. The construction of a yarn can also have a bearing. However, as none of the projects in this book are close-fitting garments or dainty projects, this isn't as crucial.

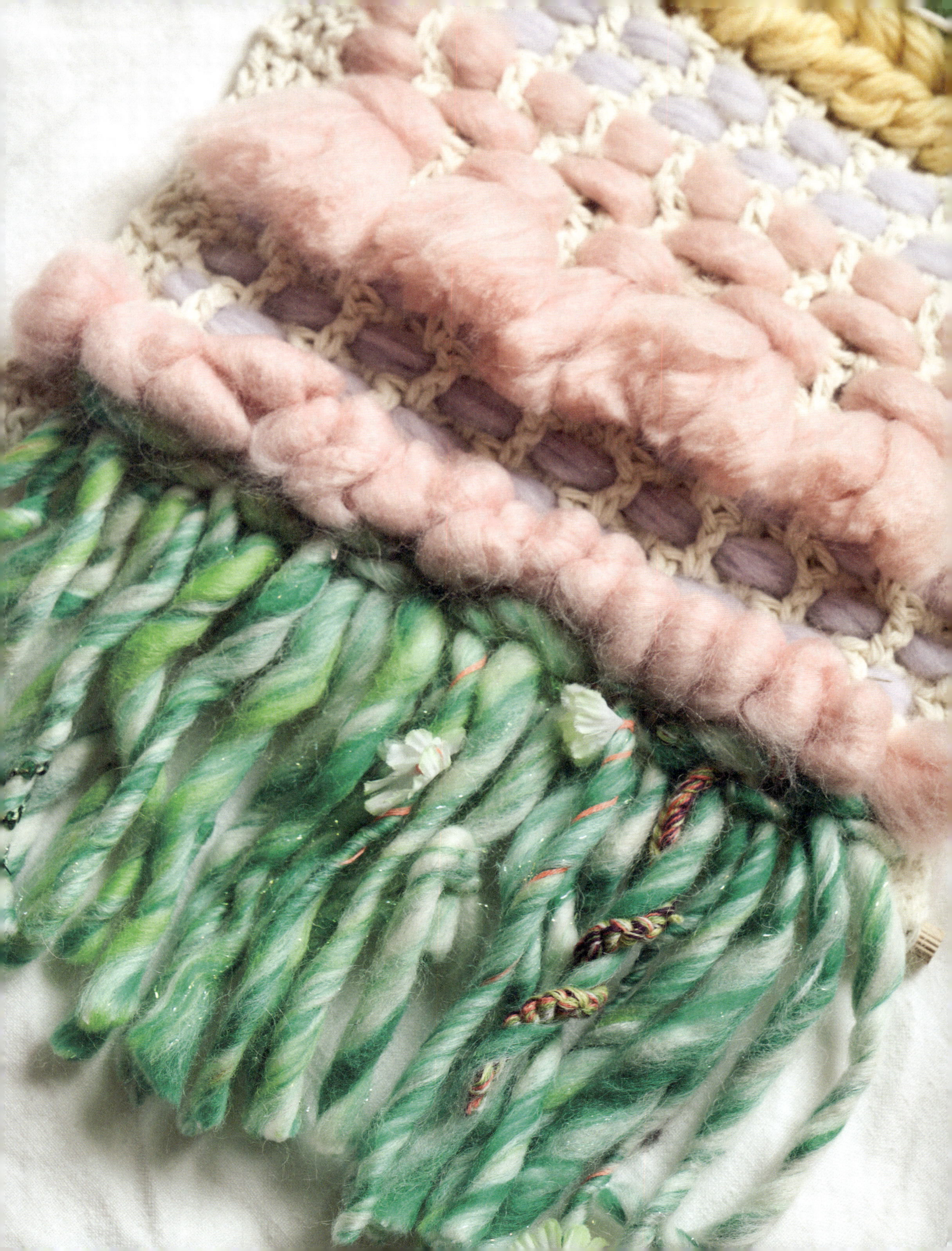

abbreviations

UK CROCHET TERMS

BBO	back bump only
BLO	back loop only
BPtr	back post treble crochet
ch	chain
ch-sp	chain-space
cm	centimetres
cs	crab stitch
dc	double crochet
dcinc	double crochet increase: make 2 double crochet stitches into 1 stitch from previous row/round
dc3inc	double crochet 2 stitches increase: make 3 double crochet stitches into 1 stitch from the previous row/round
dc2tog	double crochet 2 stitches together to decrease 1 stitch
F	foundation row/round
FLO	front loop only
FPdc	front post double crochet
FPhtr	Front post half treble crochet
FPtr	Front post treble crochet
FPtr2tog	Front post treble crochet 2 stitches together
g	gram
htr	half treble crochet
in	inch
ls	loop stitch
m	metre
ML	magic loop
mm	millimetre
PM	place stitch marker
prev	previous
rep	repeat
rnd(s)	round(s)
RS	right side
sdc	split double crochet
sk	skip the st from the row/round below
sp	space
ss	slip stitch
st(s)	stitch(es)
tr	treble crochet
wc	waistcoat stitch
WS	wrong side
yd	yard
*	repeat the instructions following the single asterisk as directed
()	work instructions within parentheses as a group of stitches all in the same stitch or space. If the parentheses include a number, eg ()x6, then the instruction inside should be repeated 6 times.
(Xsts)	the number given in parentheses at the end of a row or round denotes the number of stitches you should have in that row or round

conversions

CROCHET STITCH CONVERSIONS

UK term	US term
double crochet (dc)	single crochet (sc)
half treble (htr)	half double crochet (hdc)
treble (tr)	double crochet (dc)
double treble (dtr)	treble (tr)
triple treble (trtr)	double treble (dtr)
tension	gauge
yarn over (yo)	yarn over hook (yoh)

CROCHET HOOK CONVERSIONS

Metric	US
4mm	G-6
4.5mm	7
5mm	H-8
6mm	J-10
7mm	-
8mm	L-11
9mm	M/N-13
10mm	N/P-15

YARN WEIGHT SYMBOL & CATEGORY NAMES

0	1	2	3	4	5	6	7
LACE	SUPER FINE	FINE	LIGHT	MEDIUM	BULKY	SUPER BULKY	JUMBO
Type of Yarns in Category							
Fingering 10-count crochet thread	Sock, Fingering, Baby	Sport, Baby	DK, Light Worsted	Worsted, Afghan, Aran	Chunky, Craft, Rug	Super Bulky, Roving	Jumbo, Roving

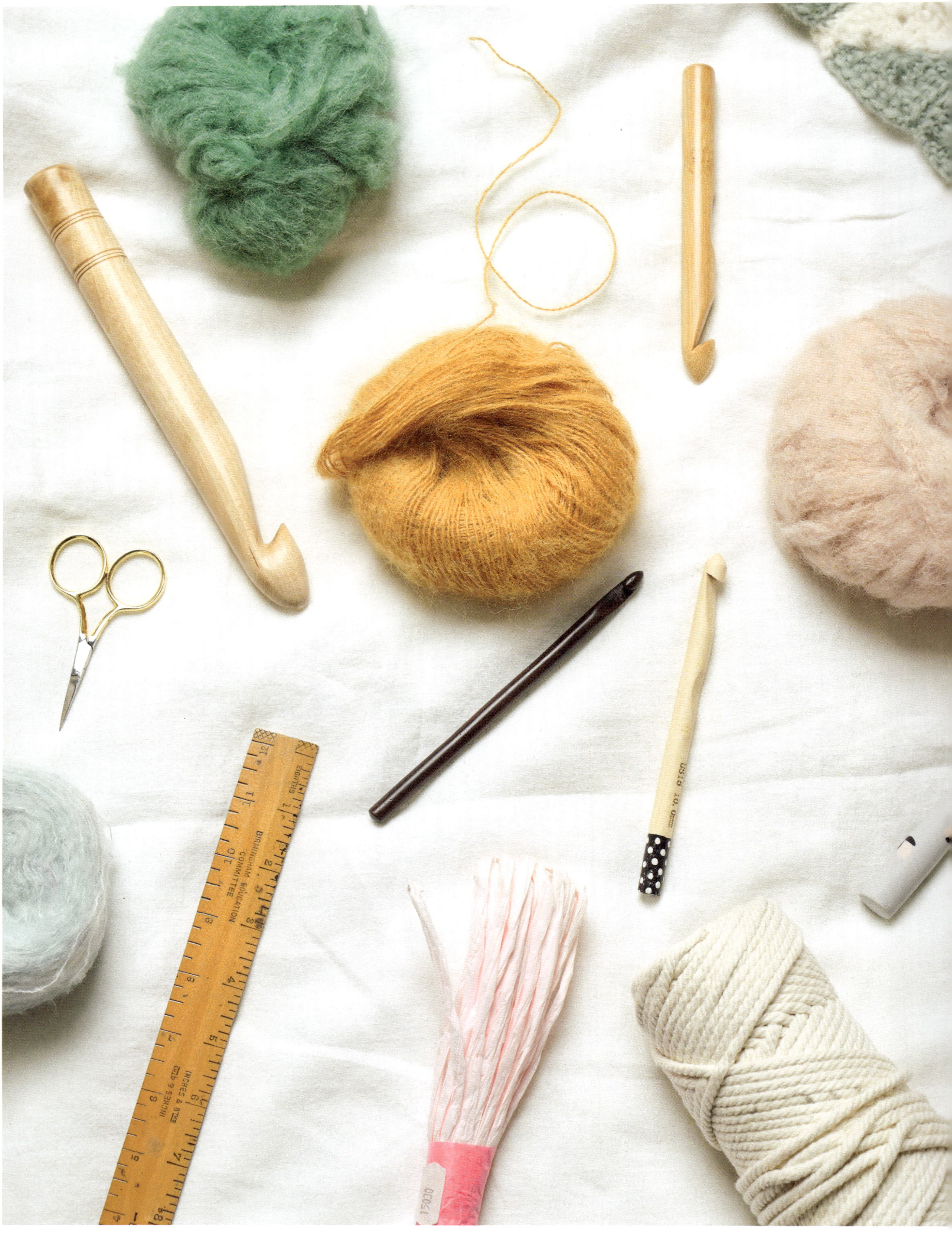
BIRMINGHAM EDUCATION COMMITTEE
15030

techniques

COMMON STITCHES

Slip Knot
Make a loop in your yarn around 10-20cm from the end. Insert hook through loop, catch the back strand of yarn, and pull it to the front. Pull the ends of the yarn to secure the knot around the hook, but not too tightly or it will be hard to pull the first loop of the chain through.

Chain (ch)
Hold the crochet hook in your hand and make a slip knot on the hook. Bring yarn over hook from back to front and pull the hook towards you to catch the loop. Pull the hooked yarn through the slip knot and onto the hook. One chain made.
Repeat these steps, keeping your stitches even, until you have the desired number of stitches. One loop will always remain on the hook.

Counting a Chain
The right side of your chain is the one that looks like a little plait of V shapes. Each V is a stitch and must be counted. When you are working the chain, do not count the slipknot, but begin to count your chain when you pull through the first loop. When you are counting after the chain has been made, count the slipknot but not the loop on the hook (the working loop).

Magic Loop (ML)
Also called the Magic Ring. This technique is frequently used when crocheting in the round and is often preferential to a ring made of chains as it allows you to pull the loop closed after your first round, meaning no small hole is left in the middle of your work. To start a magic loop, create a loop in the same way as when making a slip knot. Insert the hook into the loop, from front to back. Wrap the yarn around the hook anticlockwise and pull the yarn through the loop. Ch1 to secure the magic loop. Work the stitches as indicated into the centre of the magic loop, making sure all stitches are worked over the loop itself and the tail end. Once you have worked your first round, pull the tail of the yarn to the close the loop.

Slip Stitch (ss)
Insert hook into required stitch, yarn over hook and pull up a loop (two loops on hook), pull the loop just formed through the first loop on the hook.

Double Crochet (dc)
Insert hook into required stitch, yarn over hook and pull up a loop (two loops on hook), yarn over hook and pull through both loops.

Half Treble Crochet (htr)
Yarn over hook (two loops on hook) and insert into required stitch, yarn over hook and pull up a loop (three loops on hook), yarn over hook and pull through all three loops.

techniques

Treble Crochet (tr)
Yarn over hook (two loops on hook) and insert into required stitch, yarn over hook and pull up a loop (three loops on hook), yarn over hook and pull through two loops (two loops on hook), yarn over hook and pull through remaining two loops.

Turning Chain
A turning chain is typically worked in between rows of crochet stitches. Its purpose is to make the transition between one row of crochet and the next row while maintaining the height of each row. After you've worked a row of crochet, you typically turn the piece over and work back across. Whether this turning chain is counted as the first stitch of the row/round depends on the individual pattern, and is listed in the Tips section of each project page.

INCREASE AND DECREASE STITCHES
Double crochet increase (dcinc)
Make two double crochet stitches into one from the previous row/round. Insert hook into required stitch, yarn over hook and pull up a loop (two loops on hook), yarn over hook and pull through both loops. Repeat once more in the base of the same stitch.

Double crochet 2 stitches increase (dc3inc)
Make three double crochet stitches into one from the previous row/round: Insert hook into required stitch, yarn over hook and pull up a loop (two loops on hook), yarn over hook and pull through both loops. Repeat twice more in the base of the same stitch.

Double crochet 2 stitches together decrease (dc2tog)
Insert hook into required stitch, yarn over hook and pull up a loop (two loops on hook). Insert hook into the next stitch along, yarn over hook and pull up a loop (three loops on hook) yarn over hook and pull through all three loops.

SPECIAL STITCHES
Back Loop Only (BLO)
When looking at the top of your stitches, they will look like a < or >, and most standard stitches require you to work through both loops at the same time. Working in the back loop only (BLO) means only working in the back bar of the < or >. At the end of a row of BLO stitches, you will have a ridge of unworked loops (the front loops) running along the front of your piece.

Front Loop Only (FLO)
When looking at the top of your stitches, they will look like a < or >, and most standard stitches require you to work through both loops at the same time. Working in the front loop only (FLO) means only working in the front bar of the < or >. At the end of a row of FLO stitches, you will have a ridge of unworked loops (the back loops) running along the back of your piece.

techniques

Back Bump Only (BBO)
Also called the third loop, or the hidden loop. Working in the back bump only (BBO) is similar to working BLO or FLO stitches, but is sometimes a little fiddlier to locate the bump to work in. With your work facing you, ignore the front and back loops (the < or > stitch on top of your work) and instead look behind the stitch, on the reverse side. The back bump is the horizontal ridge running across the back of the stitch. Working in the BBO will push the front and back loops to the front of the work, creating a ribbed effect with the top > sitting on the front of the work.

Post Stitches
When working post stitches, the stitch formation is the same as normal for all stitches, double crochet, half treble crochet, trebles etc., the main difference is where the stitches are formed. Instead of working into the top < or > of the stitch, you are working around the post: the vertical body of the stitch underneath. Working post stitches pushes the stitches to either the front or the back of the work, and can be used to create ribbing, cables, or textured patterns.

Front Post Double Crochet (FPdc)
Insert hook from the front of your work to the back, around the back of the indicated post stitch and back through to the front, yarn over hook and pull round the back of the post of the indicated stitch, yarn over hook and pull through 2 loops.

Front Post Half Treble Crochet (FPhtr)
Yarn over hook, insert hook from the front of your work to the back, around the back of the indicated post stitch and back through to the front, yarn over hook and pull round the back of the post of the indicated stitch, yarn over hook and pull through 3 loops.

Front Post Treble (FPtr)
Yarn over hook, insert hook from the front of your work to the back, around the back of the indicated stitch and back through to the front, yarn over hook and pull round the back of the post of the indicated stitch, (yarn over hook and pull through 2 loops) twice.

Front Post Treble Two Together (FPtr2tog)
This stitch is used to decrease the front post treble stitch. Yarn over hook, insert hook from the front of your work to the back, around the back of the indicated stitch and back through to the front, yarn over hook and pull round the back of the post of the indicated stitch, yarn over hook and pull through 2 loops. Yarn over hook, insert hook from the front of your work to the back, around the back of the next stitch along and back through to the front, yarn over hook and pull round the back of the post of the indicated stitch, yarn over hook and pull through 2 loops. Yarn over hook and pull through all remaining loops on hook.

techniques

Back Post Treble (BPtr)
Yarn over hook, insert hook from the back of your work to the front, around the front of the indicated post stitch and back through to the back, yarn over hook and pull round the front of the post of the indicated stitch, (yarn over hook and pull through 2 loops) twice.

Crab Stitch (cs)
Working in the opposite direction to the way you normally work (for a right-hander this is to the right), double crochet as follows: Insert hook into the stitch to the right. **(Fig. 1)** Yarn under, pull up a loop. **(Fig. 2)** Yarn over hook and pull through both loops. Crab stitch formed. **(Fig. 3 & 4)**

Loop Stitch (ls)
Loop stitches are formed on the 'back' of the work and so should always be worked on Wrong Side rows. To form a loop stitch, wrap your yarn from front to back over the index finger of your yarn hand. Insert hook into stitch, and bring the yarn under the hook, keeping your finger in place. Next, grab the strand of yarn from behind your index finger, and draw the loop through the stitch, still keeping your finger in place. You should now have two loops on your hook, and a loop of yarn wrapped around your index finger. Yarn over hook as normal and pull through both loops on hook. Loop stitch is formed, and you can remove your finger.

techniques

Split Double Crochet (sdc)

This stitch is a variation on double crochet which, when used in conjunction with tapestry crochet, creates a colour change V on the front of the work. With Yarn A on hook, insert hook into stitch and yarn over hook with Yarn B. **(Fig. 5 & 6)**
Pull up a loop with Yarn B. Two loops on hook, one of each yarn. **(Fig. 7)** Yarn over hook with Yarn A (even when working a row in colour B), and pull through both loops. Split double crochet formed. **(Fig. 8 & 9)**

Standing Double Crochet

This is an alternative to ss and ch1 when joining new yarn at the start or a row. Start with a slip knot on your hook. Insert hook into indicated stitch. Yarn over hook and pull up a loop, yarn over hook and pull through both loops on your hook.

Waistcoat Stitch (wc)

Also known as knit stitch. Waistcoat stitch is a variation on double crochet, which creates a more aligned, stacked stitch than the traditional double crochet stitch, due to where the stitch is worked. When working waistcoat stitch, instead of working into the top of the stitch (< or >), you are working instead into the front of the stitch, above the V formed by the stitch in the row below. Insert hook into the stitch, placing it in the lower V of the stitch from the previous round/row. Yarn over hook and pull up a loop. Yarn over hook and pull through both loops on hook.

techniques

Whip Stitch

The whip stitch is a simple hand-sewing stitch, typically used to sew together two separate pieces of material with flat edges. It creates a visible seam.
Thread your yarn needle and make sure the two edges you want to sew together are aligned. Push your needle up through both layers (or both stitches) of the crochet edge from bottom to top. Next, bring the needle and yarn around the outside edges, and underneath to the bottom again. Sew up from bottom to top through the next crochet stitch along. Repeat this process until indicated in pattern.

Crochet Styles

Working in the round – spiral method

When working in the round, the pattern will start with a Magic Loop or a chained foundation ring. For the first round of the pattern, stitches will be made into the centre of the loop or ring.
When working the spiral method, at the end of the round no join will be made to connect the last stitch of the round to the first stitch of the round, and the work is not turned. Instead, the first stitch of round 2 will be made into the top of the first stitch of round 1. In this way, as the rounds increase and the pattern grows, the rounds create a spiral.

Using a stitch marker to mark the start/end of the round is particularly useful when working this method, as it is easy to lose your place and it is not immediately obvious where the rounds start and end.

Working in the round – join method

When working in the round, the pattern will start with a Magic Loop or a chained foundation ring. For the first round of the pattern, stitches will be made into the centre of the loop or ring.
When working the join method, at the end of the round a join will be made to connect the last stitch of the round to the first stitch of the round; this is usually a slip stitch. The work is not turned. In this way, as you move from one round to another, each round will require a ch1 (or equivalent chain to the height of the stitch you are using) to 'step up' at the start of the round to create the correct height.
Using this method creates a more obvious join than with the spiral method, but it can be more helpful when using colour work, and to create a very flat top edge to the piece.

Filet Crochet

Filet crochet is a technique which uses solid blocks of crochet in combination with open mesh made using chain stitches. The technique can be used to create patterns and pictures.

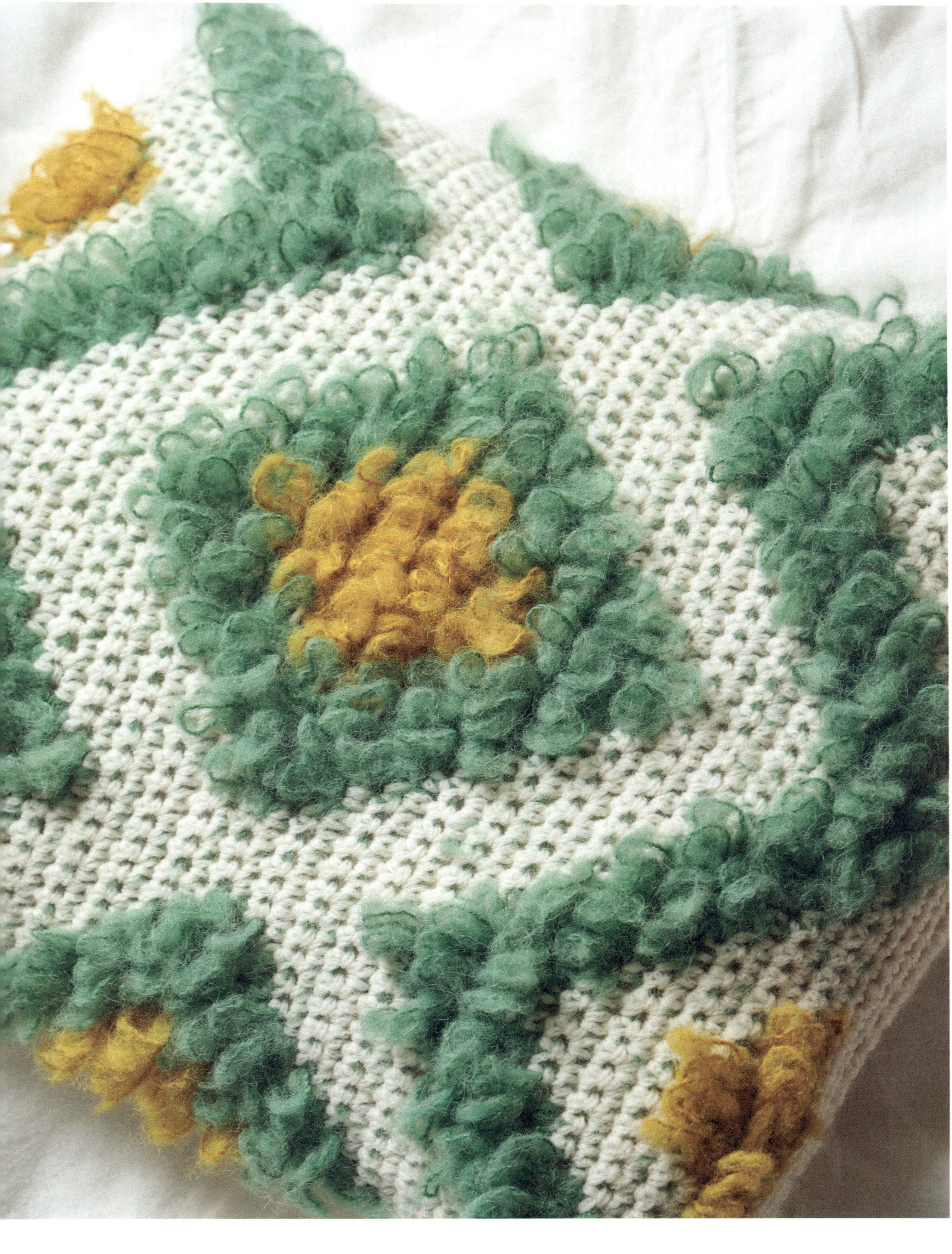

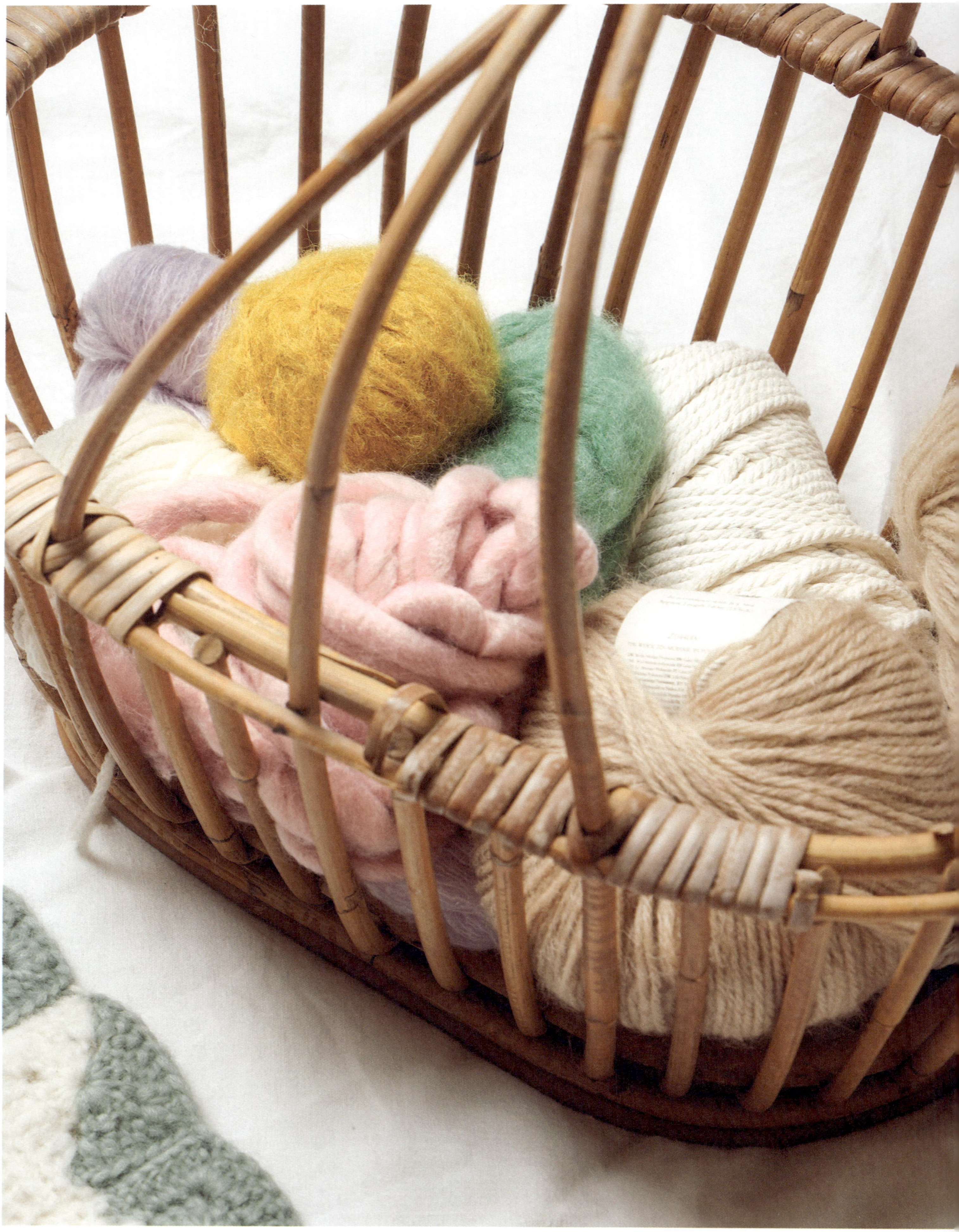

crochet colourwork

Changing colour

To create a clean colour change when switching between yarns, you will need to complete the last part of the previous stitch in your new colour. If you are following a chart or instructions, it won't explicitly show this, but you will need to work the stitch before the colour change until you have two loops left on the hook (depending on whether the stitch is double crochet, or treble crochet) or three loops on the hook (half treble crochet).

Yarn over with the new colour and pull through all the loops on your hook. The completed stitch won't show any of the new colour, but the working yarn will be ready in the new colour to create the next stitch.

Intarsia

Intarsia is a form of crochet (and knitting) colourwork that allows you to place large patches of colour into your work. Typically, because the colours are worked in blocks in this style, the non-working yarn(s) are not carried (worked over by other stitches). Instead, you will be instructed to create a small, separate ball of yarn (card bobbins or pegs are handy for winding these) for each block of colour.

When working in rows, this block of colour is then picked up when working back down the row. This style of colourwork usually has a clear right side (RS), and a wrong side (WS) where the colour changes will be more obvious, and where the tail ends of the non-working yarns will be left until needed again.

Tapestry crochet

Tapestry crochet is a colourwork technique that involves working 2 or more colours of yarn within a single row. Typically, the working colour is worked over (and covers) the non-working colour(s), so that it is hidden inside the stitches. This technique is useful when you need to swap back and forth between your colours every few stitches.

Managing yarn

To avoid getting in a tangle when working in tapestry crochet, set one ball of yarn slightly in front of you, and one slightly behind. When changing colours, always pull the yarn behind you to the front of the work, and the yarn in front of you to the back of the work, to stop them twisting as you switch between the two.

Turning neatly

Although tapestry crochet doesn't have a RS and WS as clearly as Intarsia, it is still helpful to be mindful of keeping one side as the RS when it comes to the end of each row. Choose which side is the WS and, at the end of each row, pull the non-working carried yarn(s) to this side. This will create a crisper edge on the RS of the work, and you will be able to see all the carried yarns on the edge of the WS of the work.

Fair Isle crochet

I use the term Fair Isle crochet here to refer to tapestry crochet where the non-working yarns aren't carried (worked over by other stitches), but left behind the work as floats, like Fair Isle knitting. This technique is useful when the colour changes are frequent, but where the non-working yarns can't easily be carried, due to the weight of the yarn or the type of crochet stitch used. When you colour change, try not to pull too tightly or the floats will distort the work. Where a colour change doesn't happen as frequently, work approximately every 4th stitch over the top of the other colours, to catch the floats and prevent them from getting too long.

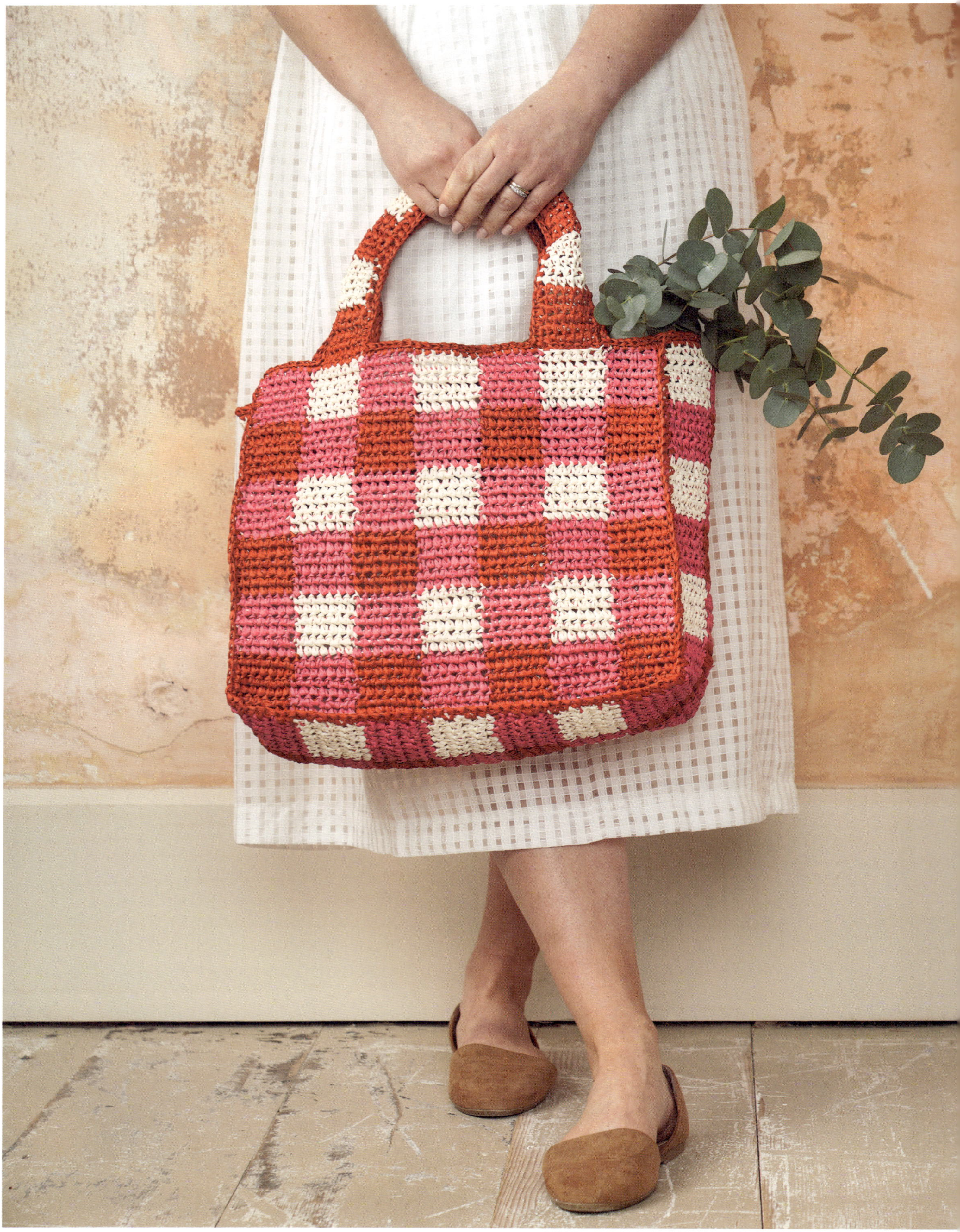

chapter one: spring

Ushering in the new growth and longer days of spring is always such a motivating time. Whether you fancy mixing up your décor, a spring clean, or making something to put a bunch of pretty blooms in, this chapter has you covered. Think plant-based yarns and fresh colours. With textured dish cloths, a woven-inspired wall hanging, luxe scrunchies and a gingham bag in gorgeous coloured raffia.

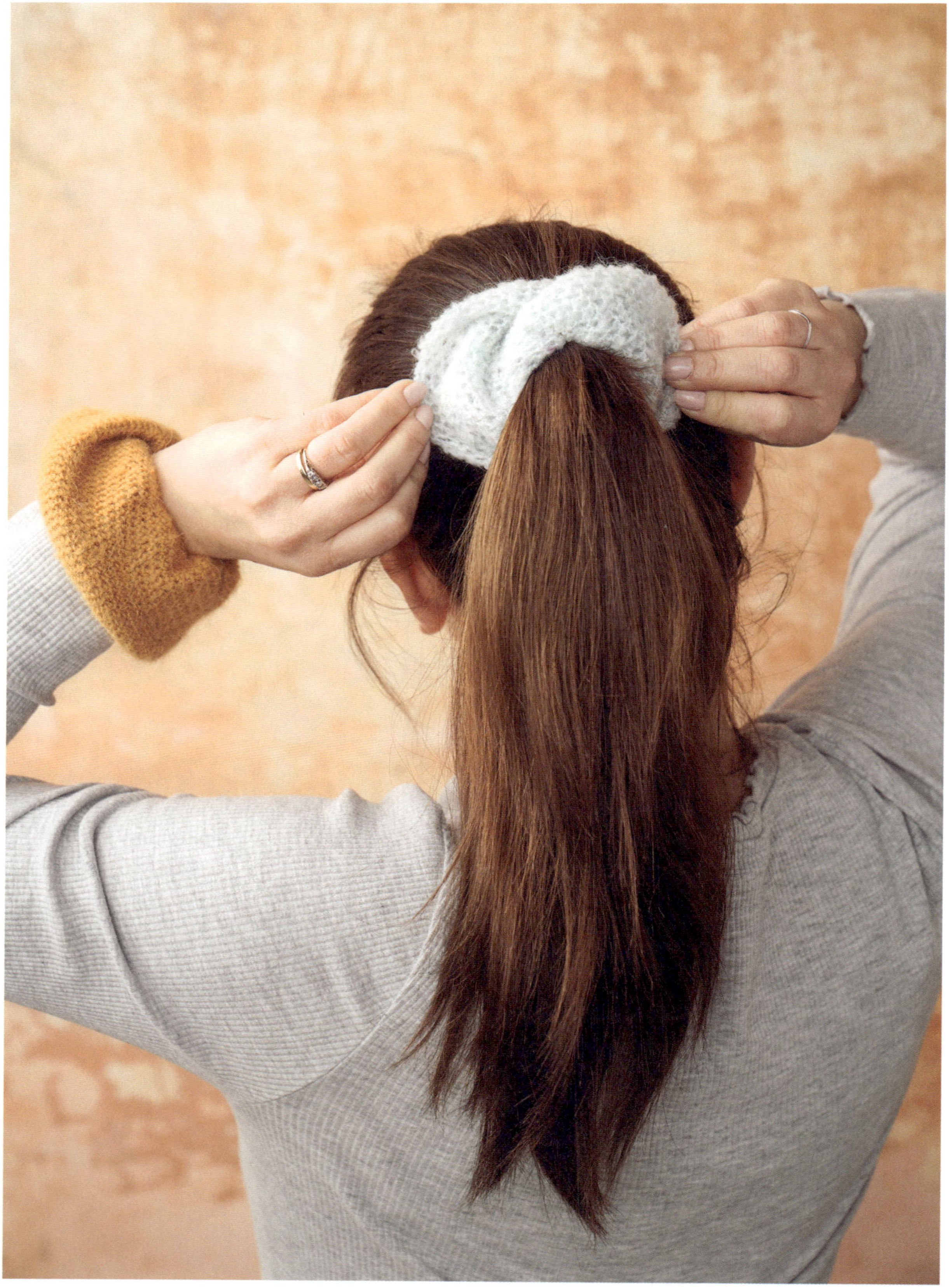

luxe scrunchies

These scrunchies are a little bit of everyday luxury. I love to use chunky and thick yarns, but sometimes it pays to have a slower and more mindful make. Using a hook size that is larger than normal for lace weight yarn gives the fabric a pretty open, airy feel.

You will need
- Lace weight Mohair, such as Rico Essentials Super Kid Mohair Loves Silk, 25g/200m/219yd, 70% Mohair/30% Silk
- 4.5mm hook
- Hair bobble (not bare elastic) approx 5cm in diameter

Yarn profile
To create a truly special scrunchie, use a fibre that has a little bit of a halo, or fluff, and look for a hand-dyed or indie yarn.

Finished size
Approx. 14cm x 14cm

Techniques – see p.12
Working in the Round – Spiral Method

Gauge
5cm x 5cm = 10sts x 13 rounds worked in dc

LINDSEY'S TIPS
- This pattern is worked in the round in a spiral. As you crochet you will encase the hair bobble in the crochet fabric.
- Due to the number of rounds, don't worry too much about marking the end/start of each round, just continue working until the scrunchie is at the desired length stated in pattern.
- As your scrunchie grows, you may need to move the hair bobble out of the way by pulling the crocheted section towards you and twisting it out of the way. Just make sure to untwist before sewing up at the end.

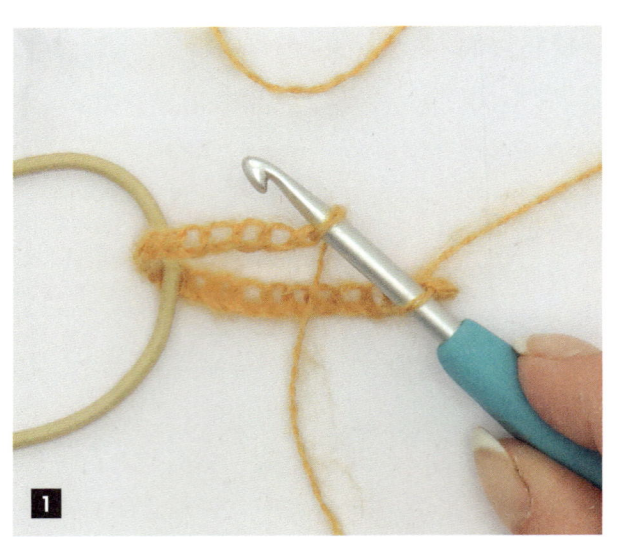

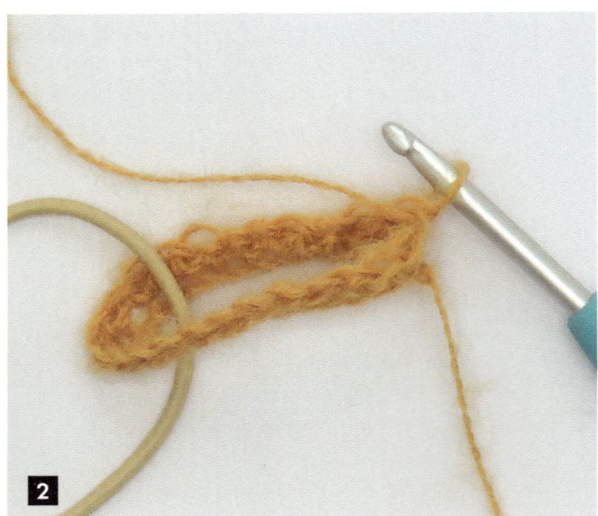

F ch25. Lay your hair bobble on top of your chain, then bring the end of your chain around to meet the hook, so that the chain is wrapped around the hair bobble to encase it. **(Fig. 1)**

Rnd 1 1dc in each chain. (25sts) **(Fig. 2)**

Rnds 2-85 25dc. **(Fig. 3)**

At this stage, your scrunchie should be bunching up in the centre, but laying nice and flat around the outside, your starting chain and the last row should meet comfortably at the outermost point of the scrunchie. If they don't, add a few more rounds until they do. **(Fig. 4)** Cut your yarn leaving a long 20cm tail, fasten off with a ss.

MAKING UP
Thread a small yarn needle with the tail end and sew the final round to the foundation chain using mattress stitch.

Step 1 Align the last round and the foundation round edges so that they sit neatly next to each other, without

CHAPTER ONE: LUXE SCRUNCHIES

twisting the body of the scrunchy. Bring the threaded yarn needle from the back of your work to the front where you want the seam to start. Start by sewing behind one of the bars of the stitch closest to the edge. **(Fig. 5)**

Step 2 Now take the needle to the opposite edge and work a stitch in this way every other rows, alternating between the two sides. Working back and forth vertically along the two edges in this way will create a ladder effect which, when pulled together, will allow the two edges to meet and create an invisible seam. **(Fig. 6)**

Step 3 Sew 10 or so rows then pull to close, repeating until you have joined the entire width of the scrunchie. Try and keep your tension even across all of your stitches, to prevent the seam puckering or gathering when you pull the mattress stitches closed. **(Fig. 7)**]

Step 4 Securing the yarn by sewing on the spot a few times, then cutting and weaving in any ends. **(Fig. 8)**

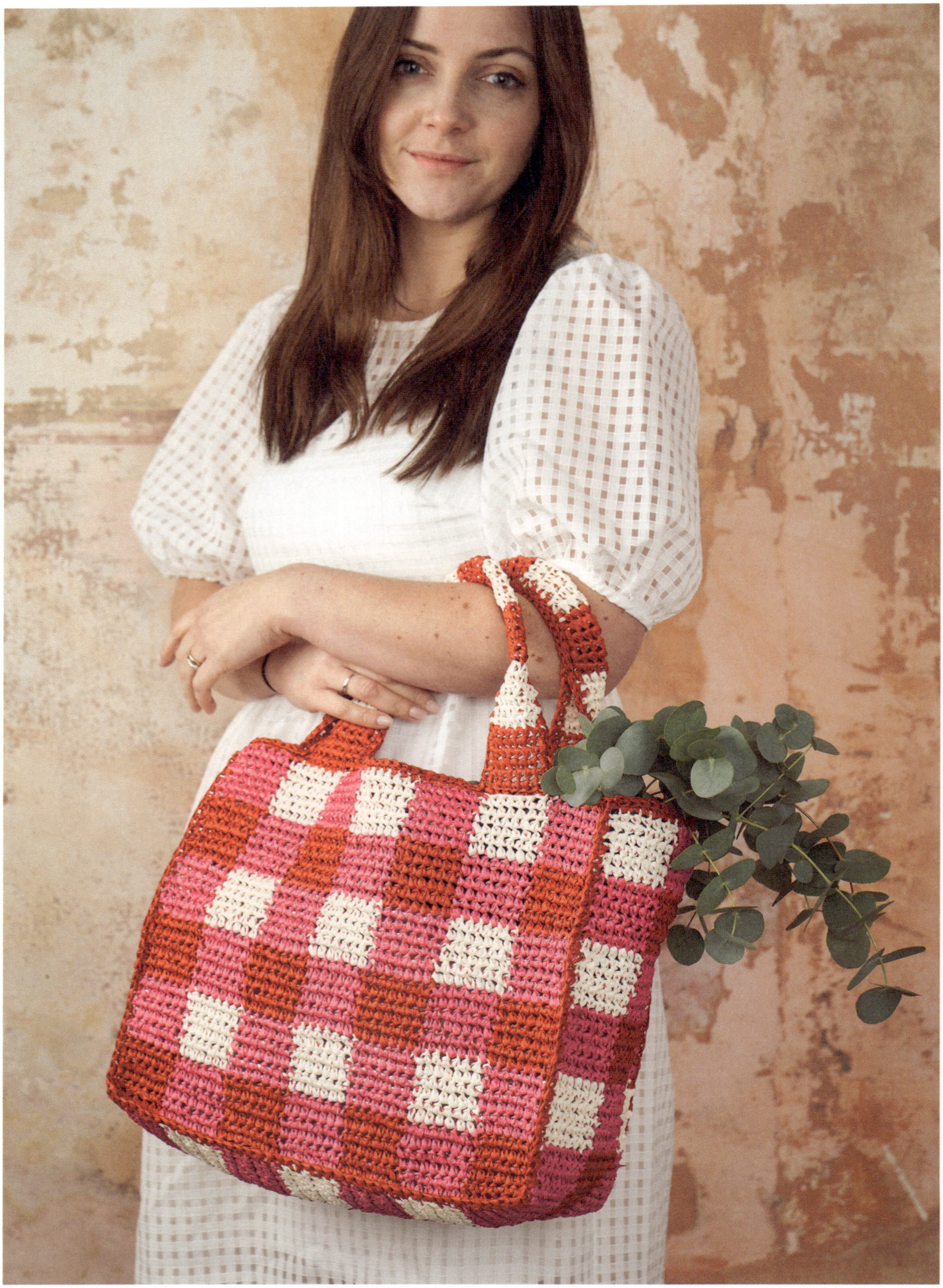

gingham bag

This bright, raffia gingham bag is just calling for a white floaty dress and a warm spring day. Don't be daunted by the tapestry crochet. You will only be working with two colours at any one time and the stitch is a super simple double crochet. The bag is made flat in three panels, joined together and the straps added.

You will need
- Wool and the Gang Ra-Ra Raffia Yarn, 100g/250m/273yd, 100% paper
  Yarn A Hot Pink x 1 roll
  Yarn B Bardot Red x 1 roll
  Yarn C Ivory White x 1 roll
- 5mm crochet hook

Yarn profile
This raffia yarn is triple treat: vegan, water-repellent and biodegradable. It's also surprisingly strong, which is great for all the fancy things you're going to want to put in your new bag.

Finished size
W50cm x H30cm x D15cm (excluding straps)

Techniques – see p.12
Crochet Colourwork
Tapestry Crochet
Whip Stitch

Gauge
10cm x 10cm = 15sts x 12 rows, worked in pattern

LINDSEY'S TIPS
- Turning chain does not count as a stitch throughout.
- Yarn A will be used or carried throughout, bringing in and fastening off Yarn B and C every 6 rows.
- Where the pattern reads 7dcB – this should be read as 7 double crochet in Yarn B, and so on.

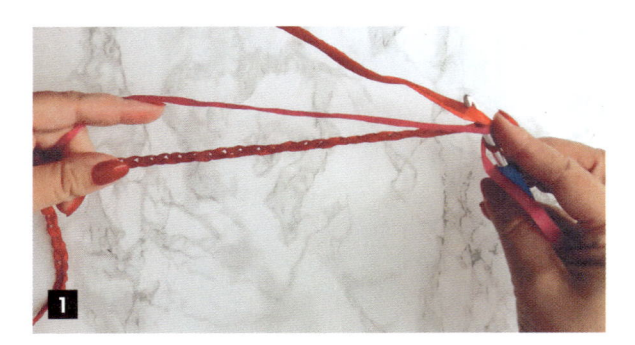

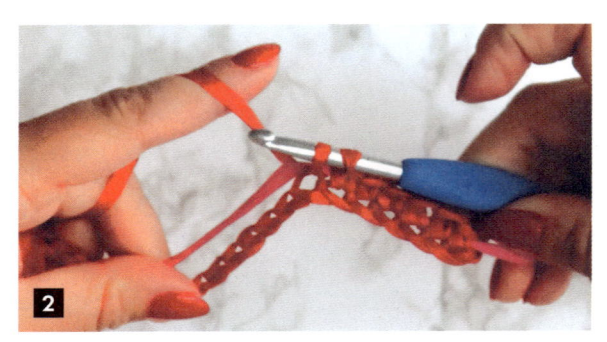

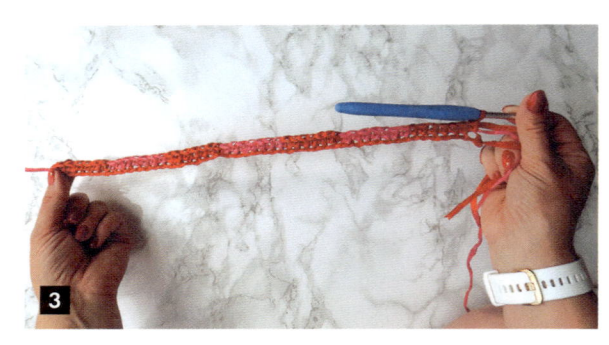

PATTERN

Side panel - make 2

F In Yarn B, ch50. Bring in Yarn A and hold on top of chain, on the next row you will be crocheting over the top of Yarn A until stated otherwise. **(Fig. 1)**

Row 1 Starting in 2nd ch from hook, 7dcB, *7dcA, 7dcB; rep from * until end, turn. (49sts) **(Fig. 2 & 3)**

Row 2 ch1, 7dcB, *7dcA, 7dcB; rep from * until end, turn.

Rows 3-6 Rep row 2. At the end of row 6, colour change to Yarn A, fasten off Yarn B, bring in Yarn C.

Row 7 In Yarn A, carrying Yarn C, ch1, 7dcA, *7dcC, 7dcA; rep from * until end, turn.

Rows 8-12 Rep row 7. At the end of row 12, bring in and colour change to Yarn B, fasten off Yarn C.

Rows 13-18 Rep row 2. At the end of row 18, colour change to Yarn A, fasten off Yarn B, bring in Yarn C.

Rows 19-24 Rep row 7. At the end of row 24, bring in and colour change to Yarn B, fasten off Yarn C.

Rows 25-30 Rep row 2. At the end of row 30, colour change to Yarn A, fasten off Yarn B, bring in Yarn C.

Rows 31-36 Rep row 7. Fasten off all colours. **(Fig. 4)**

Base – make 1

Note pattern is not continuous in this section, see rows 31-42 and 73-84. This is to allow the pattern to match on the sides and the base as it curves round the corner of the bag when making up.

F In Yarn C, ch22.

Bring in Yarn A and hold on top of F, crocheting over the top until needed.

Row 1 Starting in 2nd ch from hook, 7dcC, 7dcA, 7dcC, turn. (21sts)

Row 2 ch1, 7dcC, 7dcA, 7dcC, turn.

Rows 3-6 Rep row 2. At the end of row 6, change colour to Yarn A, fasten off Yarn C, bring in Yarn B.

Row 7 ch1, 7dcA, 7dcB, 7dcA, turn.

Rows 8-12 Rep row 7. At the end of row 7, bring in

CHAPTER ONE: GINGHAM BAG

and colour change to Yarn C, fasten off Yarn B.
Rows 13-18 Rep row 2. Continue to change colour as required when changing pattern Rows from 2 to 7 and 7 to 2
Rows 19-24 Rep row 7.
Rows 25-30 Rep row 2.
Rows 31-42 Rep row 7.
Rows 43-48 Rep row 2. **(Fig. 5)**
Rows 49-54 Rep row 7.
Rows 55-60 Rep row 2.
Rows 61-66 Rep row 7.
Rows 67-72 Rep row 2.
Rows 73-84 Rep row 7.
Rows 85-90 Rep row 2.
Rows 91-96 Rep row 7.
Rows 97-102 Rep row 2.
Rows 103-108 Rep row 7.
Rows 109-114 Rep row 2.
Fasten off all colours. **(Fig. 6)**

Straps – make 2
With side panel facing right side up, join Yarn B, carrying Yarn C, to the 8th dc from the right-hand edge. Change colour from Yarn B to C every 6 rows, carrying the yarn not being worked with.
Row 1 8dcB, turn. (8sts)
Rows 2-6 ch1, 8dcB, turn. At the end of row 6, colour change to Yarn C and carry Yarn B.
Rows 7-12 ch1, 8dcC, turn. At the end of row 12, colour change to Yarn B and carry Yarn C.
Rows 13-18 Rep row 2. **(Fig. 7)**
Rows 19-24 Rep row 7.
Rows 25-30 Rep row 2.
Rows 31-36 Rep row 7.
Rows 37-42 Rep row 2.
Rows 43-48 Rep row 7.
Rows 49-52 Rep row 2.
Fasten off all colours, leaving a long tail of Yarn B. Using yarn needle and Yarn B, whip stitch Row 52 to the side panel of your bag, 8dc from the end, so that

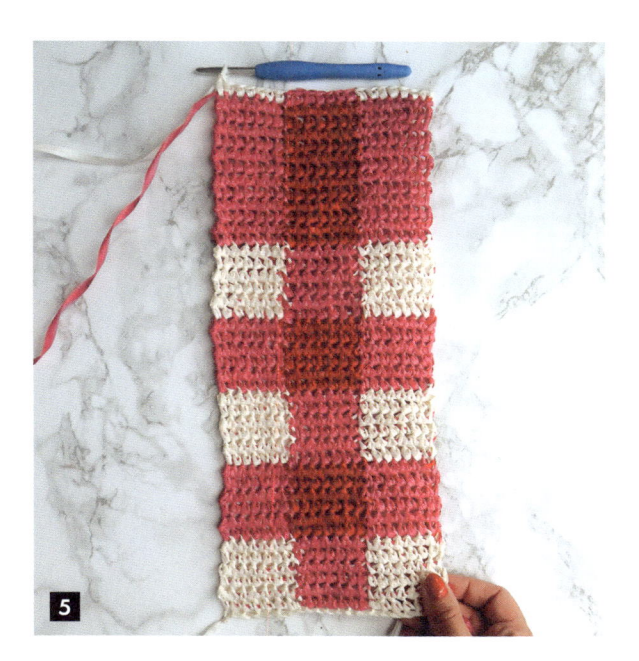

31

MODERN CROCHET STYLE

CHAPTER ONE: GINGHAM BAG

it sits on top of the last Yarn C section. **(Fig. 8)**

Repeat for second panel.

MAKING UP
With 1 side panel and base held wrong sides together, crochet together around the outside edge using dc and Yarn B. The stitches should sit on the outside of the work, for a visible join.
Step 1 Starting at top-right corner of side panel, working through both pieces, work 36dc down side, 2dc in corner, 42dc along bottom edge, 2dc in corner, 36dc up the other side. Fasten off.
(Fig. 9 & 10 opposite)
Step 2 Repeat for second side panel.
Step 3 Reattach Yarn B at top right corner of side panel. Work 7dc to strap, 12dc up the outside of strap. At 2nd Yarn B section of strap, fold the strap down the centre and work dc through both outside edges of the strap, so that they join together on the reverse of the strap. Work 30dc through both edges, then 12dc along outside edge of strap only, 7dc along left top of bag, 18dc along top base panel of bag. Do not fasten off but continue along top of second side panel. **(Fig. 11)**
Step 4 Repeat for second side panel. Fasten off.
Step 5 Reattach Yarn B on the inside of the bag strap, at row 12 (just below where the strap doubles). Work 12dc down to the top of the bag, 21dc across top of bag, 12dc up the inside of the other end of the strap. Fasten off.
Step 6 Repeat for second strap on side panel. Fasten off and weave in all ends.
Step 7 Reattach Yarn B at top right corner of side panel, into the last Yarn B dc made. Rep Steps 3-6 using ss instead of dc, so that the sts sit raised on the front of all the edging, to mirror the bag's base seam join. **(Fig. 12)**
Fasten off by cutting yarn and ss, weave in all ends.

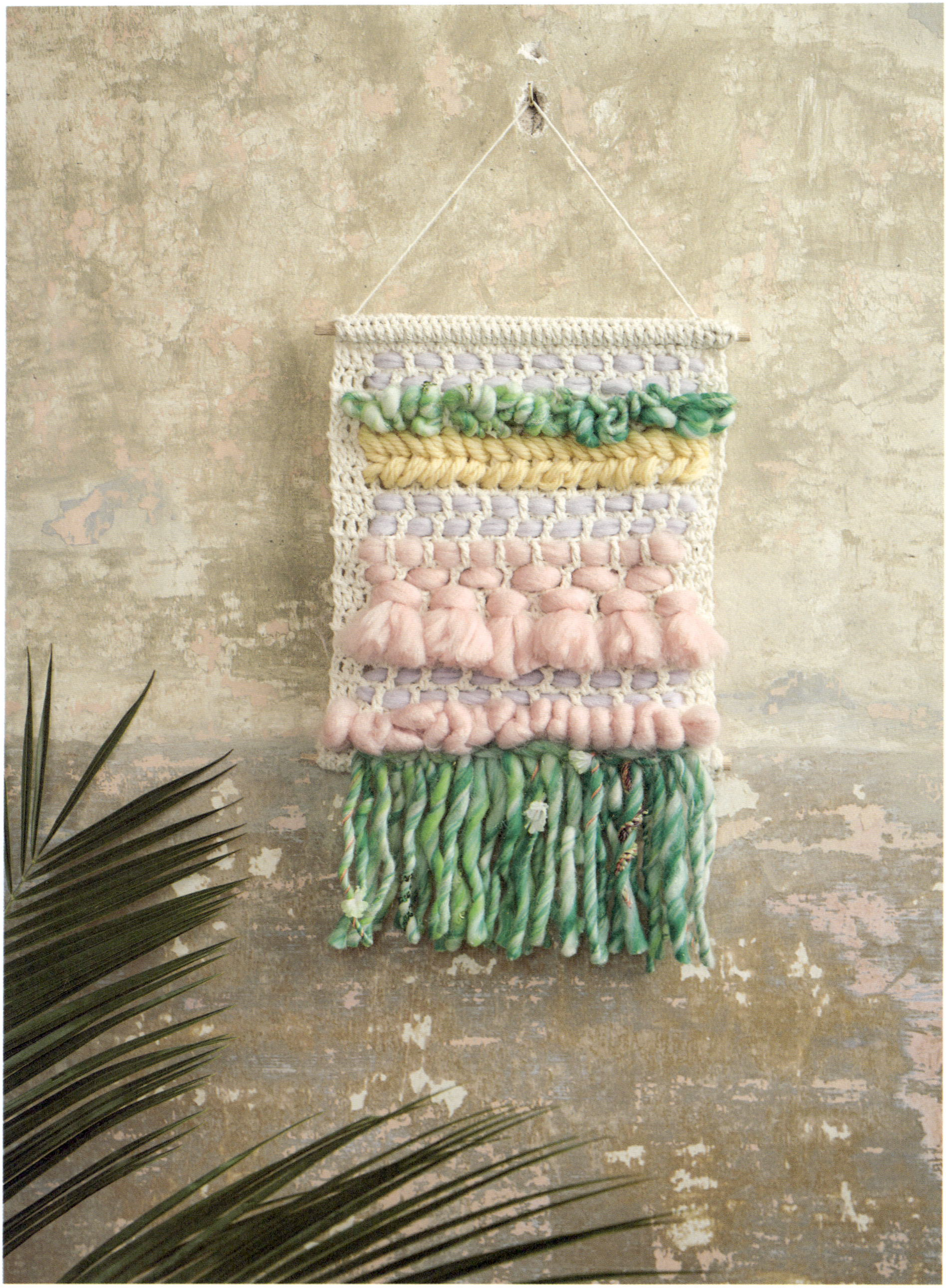

woven wallhanging

I love combining craft techniques, and this little weave brilliantly does just that. Instead of weaving on a loom, we will start with a crochet base. You can then weave and tie your most special yarns to showcase them. They deserve to be seen every day, after all, don't they?

You will need
- Rico Creative Cotton Aran, 50g/85m/93yd, 100% cotton
  Yarn A Nature (60) x1 ball
- Selection of scrap yarns – chunky and super chunky yarns (or thinner yarns with multiple strands held together) work best
  Yarn B Aran weight yarn in lilac
  Yarn C Chunky yarn in green
  Yarn D Chunky yarn in yellow
  Yarn E Super Chunky yarn in pink
- 5mm crochet hook
- 2 x 25cm lengths of 5mm wooden dowel

Yarn profile
The cotton yarn for this weave provides strength and stability.

Finished size
H30cm x W22cm

Techniques – see p.12
Filet Crochet
Front Loop Only
Back Loop Only
Whip Stitch

LINDSEY'S TIPS
- Turning chains do count as stitches throughout, so the last stitch of every row will be into the top of a chain 3.

PATTERN
Crochet base (Fig.1)

F using Yarn A ch42, leaving a 30cm tail end.
Row 1 starting in 4th chain from hook, 39tr, turn. (40sts)
Row 2 ch3, 39tr, turn.
Row 3 ch3, working in FLO for this row only, 1tr, *1tr, ch1, sk 1st; rep from * 16 more times, 4tr, turn.
Row 4 ch3, 1tr, *1tr, ch1, sk1st; rep from * 16 more times, 4tr, turn.
Rows 5-19 rep row 4.
Row 20 ch3, working in BLO of sts and chs for this row only, 39tr, turn.
Row 21 ch3, 39tr.
Cut yarn leaving a long 30cm tail end, and fasten off with a ss.

MODERN CROCHET STYLE

RYA KNOTS

1

2

3

4

WEAVE TECHNIQUES
Rya Knots

Fold a length of yarn in half and place the midpoint on top of one chain space **(Fig. 1)**, wrap the ends of the yarn around the two trebles and into the chain spaces either side, to the back of the work. **(Fig. 2)** Finally, pull the two ends to the front through the middle chain space, pull gently to tighten. **(Fig. 3 and Fig. 4)**

CHAPTER ONE: WOVEN WALLHANGING

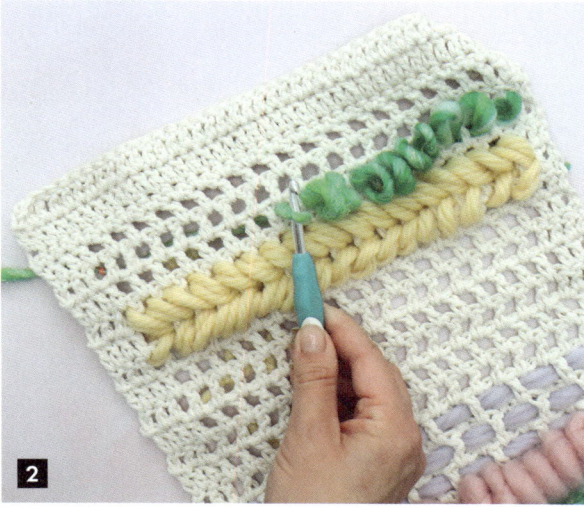

LOOPS

TABBY WEAVE

LOOPS
Holding a length of yarn firmly behind the work, insert a crochet hook into the first chain space and yarn over hook, then pull up a loop to the front of the work, without pulling the yarn tail all the way through to the front.
(Fig. 1) Remove your crochet hook, leaving your loop in place. If your loop does not stay put, double or triple up your yarn to create a thicker loop. Repeat in the next chain space a long, or in every 2nd/3rd chain space etc., depending on the thickness of your yarn. **(Fig. 2)**

TABBY WEAVE
(Fig. 3) Cut a length of yarn 2-3 times as wide as your crochet weave, then thread your yarn onto a large yarn needle. Starting from the back of the work, weave the yarn in and out of the chain spaces. If when you reach the end of the row you are on top of the work, come down on the other side of the nearest treble.

37

SOUMAK

(Fig. 1) A soumak is made by weaving diagonally from the first row into the second row below, then diagonally in the opposite direction from the second to third row. Choose 3 rows to work across and start top left. Bring your yarn to the front of the work in row 1, then down to the back of the work in row 2, choosing a chain space that is not directly below, but on a diagonal. Repeat till the end of the rows 1 and 2.

(Fig. 2) To make the second line, start on the far right of row 2, and bring your yarn to the front of the work, then down to the back of the work through a chain space in row 3. Work diagonally along rows 2-3 in the opposite direction to rows 1-2.

WEAVE PATTERN

Using your crochet as a base with the unworked loops of Rows 3 and 20 on the Wrong Side of the work, weave as follows:

Row 3 In Yarn C, cut 17 x 35cm lengths and make a rya knot in every ch-sp. Trim knot ends to 12cm.
Row 4 In Yarn E, create a loop in each ch-sp.
Rows 5-7 In Yarn B cut 3 x 2m lengths and hold triple, tabby weave.
Row 8 In Yarn E, tabby weave.
Row 9 In Yarn E, cut 11 x 15cm lengths. Place 6 rya knots in evenly across the row. Trim knots ends to 3cm.
Rows 10-11 In Yarn E, tabby weave.

CHAPTER ONE: WOVEN WALLHANGING

MAKING UP

1

Row 12-13 In Yarn B cut 3 x 2m lengths and hold triple, tabby weave.
Rows 14-16 In Yarn D cut 2 x 1m lengths, create a soumak over these 3 rows.
Row 17 In Yarn C, cut 2 x 1m lengths and hold double, create a loop in every ch-sp.
Rows 18-19 In Yarn B held triple, tabby weave.

2

MAKING UP
Step 1 Once your weave is complete, secure any ends on the back of your work by tucking them in or tying off and cutting. Leave the two long crochet tail ends.
Step 2 (Fig. 1) Place your weave wrong-side up, and lay the two wooden dowels on top of crochet rows 1-2 and 20-21. Using the long yarn tail, whip stitch through each stitch on row 1 to the unworked loops from row 3, encasing the dowel inside these two rows.
Step 3 Repeat for row 21 and the unworked loops from row 20. Secure ends by weaving in and trimming any excess. **(Fig. 2)**
Step 4 Finally, tie a 30cm piece of yarn to either end of the top dowel to hang your weave from.

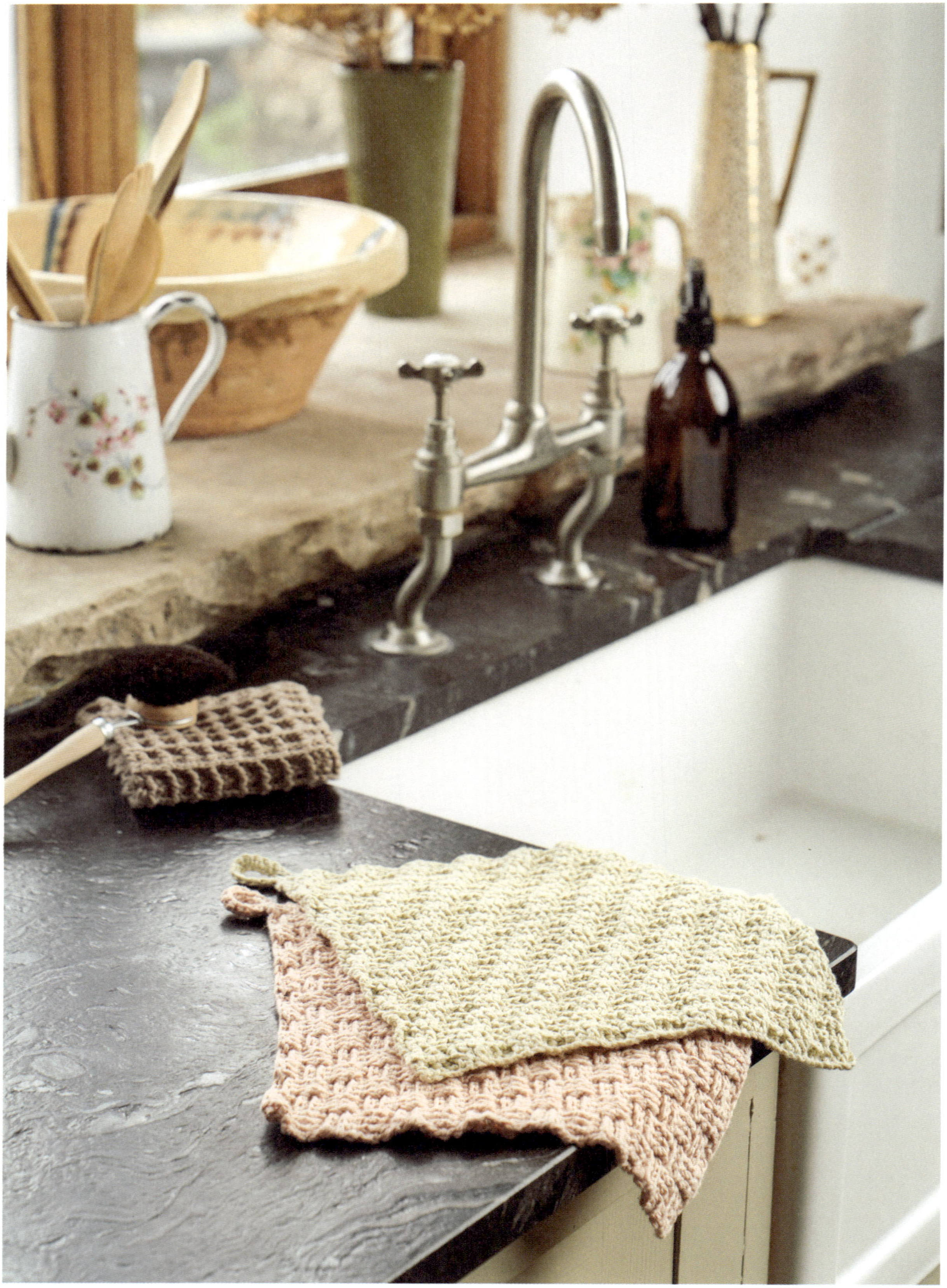

textured cloths

These deliciously textured cloths will not only look beautiful hanging in your kitchen, but their patterns make them ideal scrub buddies. These basket weave, waffle and herringbone patterns all use very similar stitches, but the order you place them in makes for totally different designs.

You will need
- Wool and the Gang Buddy Hemp Yarn, 100g/174m/190yd, 55% Hem/45% Organic Cotton
  Yarn A Timberwolf x 1 ball
  Yarn B Cameo Rose x 1 ball
  Yarn C Pistachio Green x 1 ball
- 5mm hook
- 4mm hook

Yarn profile
Made in hemp yarn, this hardwearing fibre will wash well, absorb lots of liquid and keep its shape as it has little stretch. Hemp is a brilliant plant as it requires little water to grow and can be replanted in the same field year after year.

Finished size
25cm x 25cm

Techniques – see p.12
Post Stitches

Gauge
10cm x 10cm = 20sts x 13 rows worked in FPtr and BPtr pattern

LINDSEY'S TIPS
- Turning chain 2 counts as a stitch throughout, for all three cloths. As such, the last stitch of each row is the turning chain (ch2) and you must work into this as a stitch.
- Each cloth pattern has a plain treble crochet at the beginning and end of each row.

BASKET WEAVE CLOTH

1

2

HERRINGBONE CLOTH

1

2

3

PATTERN

Basket Weave Cloth – in Yarn B **(Fig. 1)**
F using a 5mm hook, ch51.
Row 1 using a 4mm hook, 1tr in 3rd ch from hook, and in each ch along, turn. (50sts)
Row 2 ch2, *3FPtr, 3BPtr; rep from * until 1st remains, 1tr, turn. **(Fig. 2)**
Row 3 rep row 2.
Row 4 ch2, *3BPtr, 3FPtr; rep from * until 1st remains, 1tr, turn.
Row 5 rep row 4.
Rows 6-29 rep rows 2-5 6 times.
Do not fasten off, see Making Up.

Herringbone Cloth – in Yarn C **(Fig. 1)**
F using a 5mm hook, ch51.
Row 1 using a 4mm hook, 1tr in 3rd ch from hook, and in each ch along, turn. (50sts)
Row 2 ch2, *3FPtr, 3BPtr; rep from * until 1st remains, 1tr, turn. **(Fig. 2)**
Row 3 ch2, 2FPtr, *3BPtr, 3FPtr; rep from * until 5sts remain, 3BPtr, 1FPtr, 1tr, turn. **(Fig. 3)**
Row 4 ch2, 2BPtr, *3FPtr, 3BPtr; rep from * until 5sts remain, 3FPtr, 1BPtr, 1tr, turn.
Row 5 ch2, *3BPtr, 3FPtr; rep from * until 1st remains, 1tr, turn.
Row 6 ch2, 1FPtr, *3BPtr, 3FPtr; rep from * until 6sts

CHAPTER ONE: TEXTURED CLOTHS

WAFFLE CLOTH

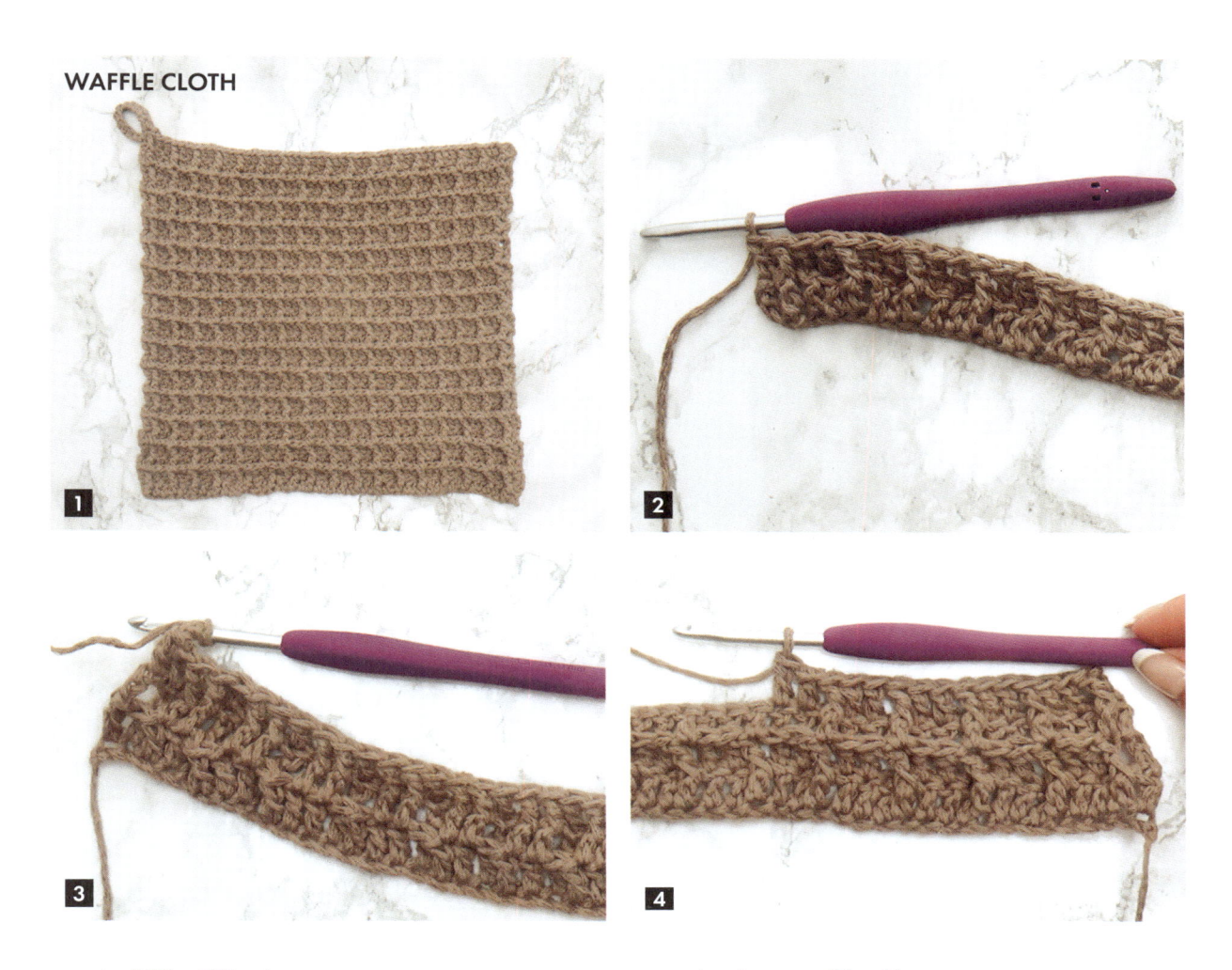

remain, 3BPtr, 2FPtr, 1tr, turn.
Row 7 ch2, 1BPtr, *3FPtr, 3BPtr; rep from * until 6sts remain, 3FPtr, 2BPtr, 1tr, turn.
Rows 8-19 rep rows 2-7 twice.
Do not fasten off, see Making Up.

Waffle Cloth – in Yarn A **(Fig. 1)**
F using a 5mm hook, ch52.
Row 1 using a 4mm hook, 1tr in 3rd ch from hook, and in each ch along, turn. (51sts)
Row 2 ch2, FPtr, *2tr, FPtr; rep from * until 1st remains, 1tr, turn. **(Fig. 2)**
Row 3 ch2, 1tr, *2FPtr, 1tr; rep from * until 1st remains, 1tr, turn. **(Fig. 3)**
Rows 4-28 rep rows 2-3. **(Fig. 4)**
Do not fasten off, see Making Up.

MAKING UP
Add a hanging loop to your cloth.
Step 1. Turn work and ss into top of last stitch made, turn. (1st)
Step 2 Ch10, and ss into the side of the last full row made, turn. (11sts)
Step 3 10dc back along chain, ss into last stitch made in cloth and fasten off. (11sts)
Fasten off and weave in all ends.

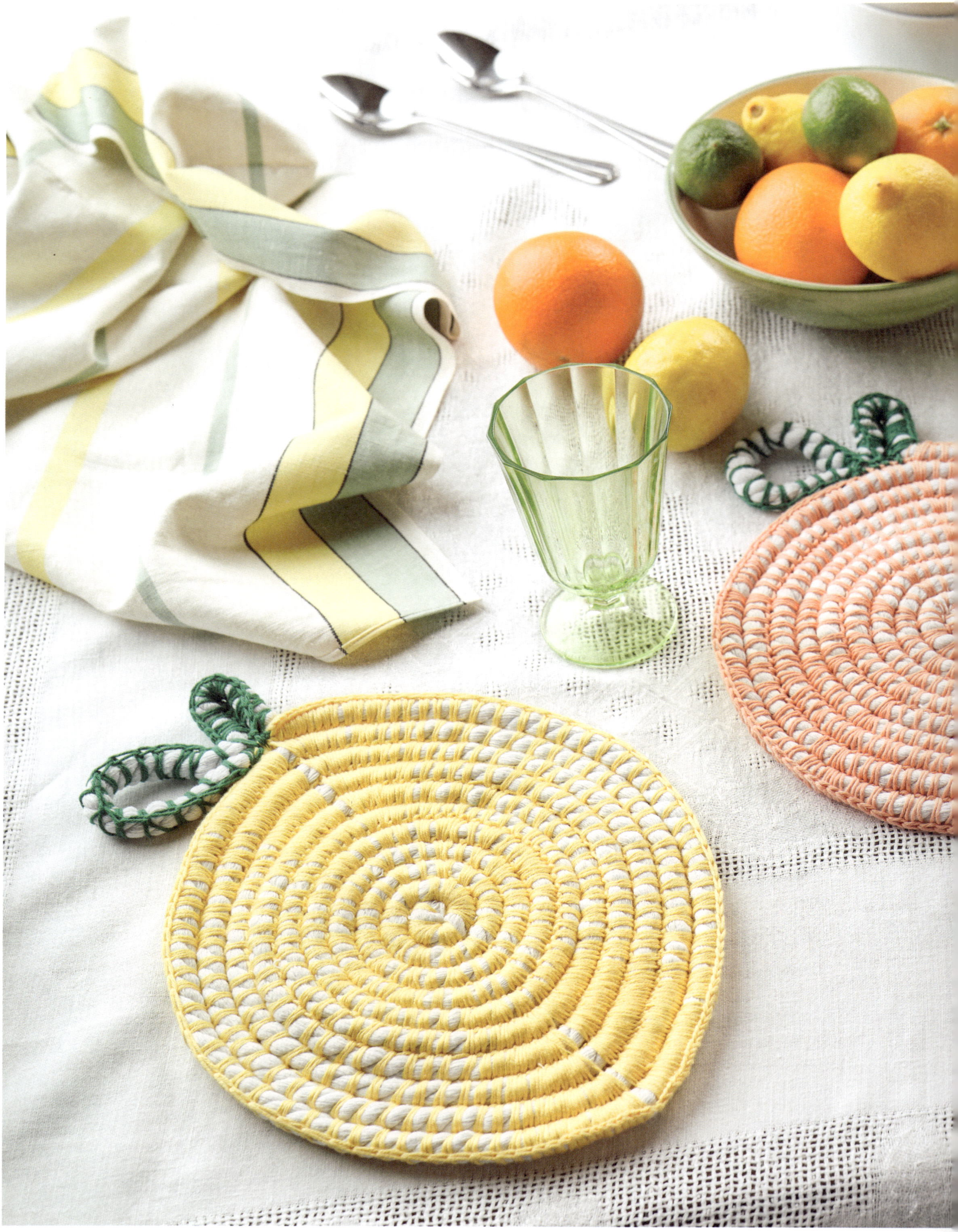

chapter two: summer

Did you think crochet was just for the colder months? Summer has plenty to keep us busy with cooler, cotton yarns and bright bursts of colour as inspiration. Treat yourself to an al-fresco breakfast on citrus fruit placemats and a Matisse-inspired eye mask for those weekend lie-ins. Or hook up boho homewares, with a tasselled basket and a loopy cushion to choose from.

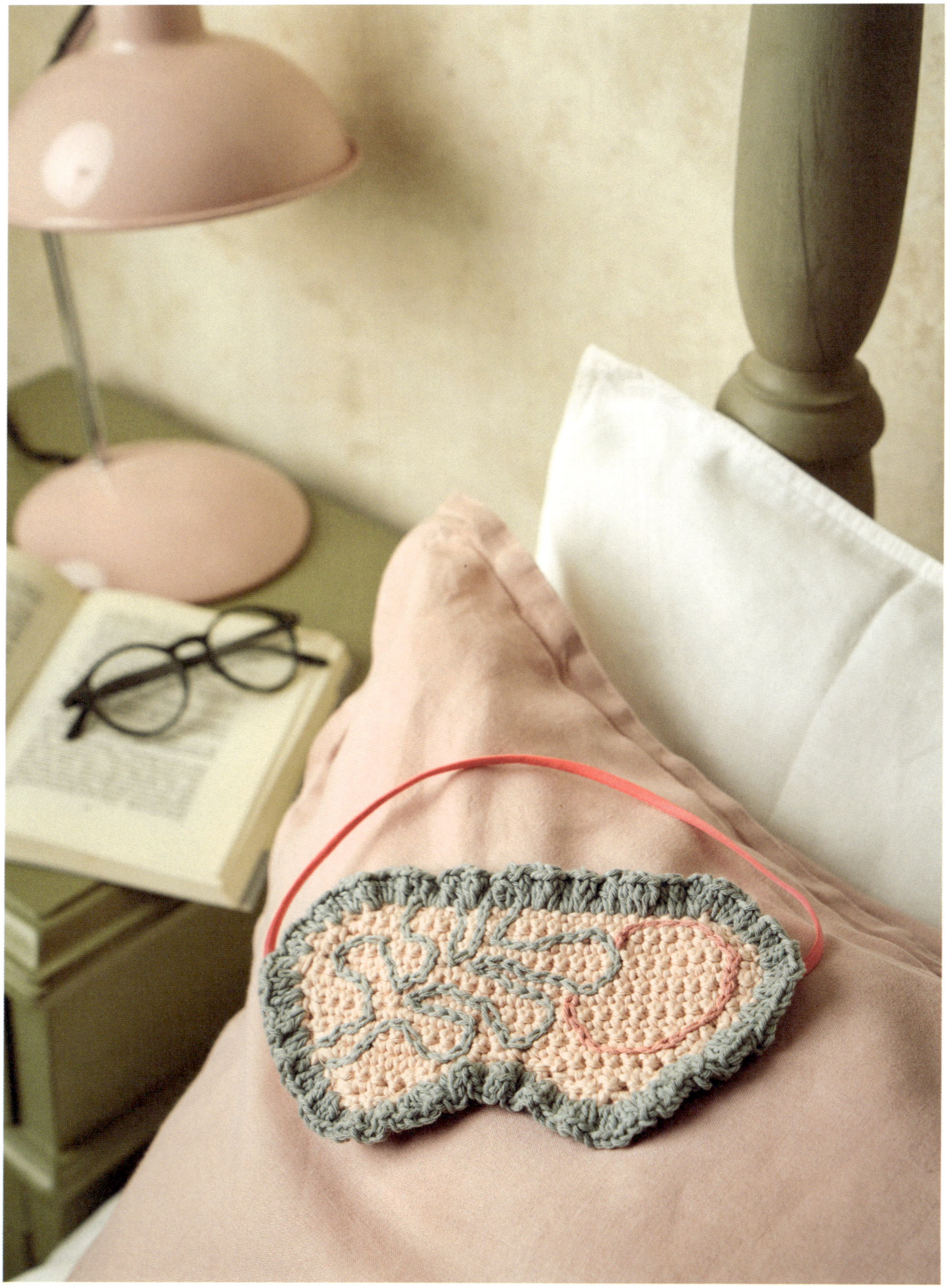

matisse eye mask

This Matisse-inspired eye mask is a little bit of fun. The fluid forms and frilly edge are softened by the calm colour palette. The design is added using surface crochet, which I think is the unsung hero of crochet. If you love the effect of embroidery but are much happier wielding a hook than a needle, then this technique is for you.

You will need
- Wool and The Gang Shiny Happy Cotton, 100% Cotton, 100g/142m/155 yd, Aran weight
  Yarn A Cameo Rose x 1 ball.
- Rico Design Ricorumi DK, 100% cotton, 25g/57.4m/63yd
  Yarn B Aqua (074) x 1 ball
  Yarn C Smokey Rose (010) x 1 ball
- 4mm crochet hook
- 1m nylon-covered elastic (I used Colour Pop 4mm elastic in pink)
- Sewing needle and thread
- 2 dressmaking pins

Yarn profile
Made using 100% cotton yarns which are breathable, soft against the skin and can be washed easily.

Finished size
H10cm x W20cm

Gauge
Not essential

LINDSEY'S TIP
- Turning chains do not count as stitches.

PATTERN
Base – make 2
F using Yarn A, ch23.
Row 1 RS starting in 2nd ch from hook, dc in each ch along, turn. (22sts)
Row 2 ch1, dcinc, 20dc, dcinc, turn. (24sts)
Row 3 ch1, dcinc, 22dc, dcinc, turn. (26sts)
Row 4 ch1, dcinc, 24dc, dcinc, turn. (28sts)
Rows 5-7 ch1, 28dc, turn. (28sts)
Row 8 ch1, dc2tog, 24dc, dc2tog, turn. (26sts)
Row 9 ch1, dc2tog, 22dc, dc2tog, turn. (24sts)
Row 10 ch1, dc2tog, 20dc, dc2tog, turn. (22sts)
Row 11 ch1, dc2tog, 6dc, dc2tog, turn. Leave rest of row unworked. (8sts)
Row 12 ch1, dc2tog, 4dc, dc2tog, turn. (6sts)
Row 13 ch1, dc2tog, 2dc, dc2tog, turn. Cut yarn and fasten off with a ss. (4sts)
Return to Row 11 and reattach yarn: leave a gap of 4sts unworked in the middle of the mask, joining to the 5th stitch from end of row 11, ch1, dc2tog, 6dc, dc2tog, turn. (8sts)
Rows 14-15 rep rows 12-13.

MODERN CROCHET STYLE

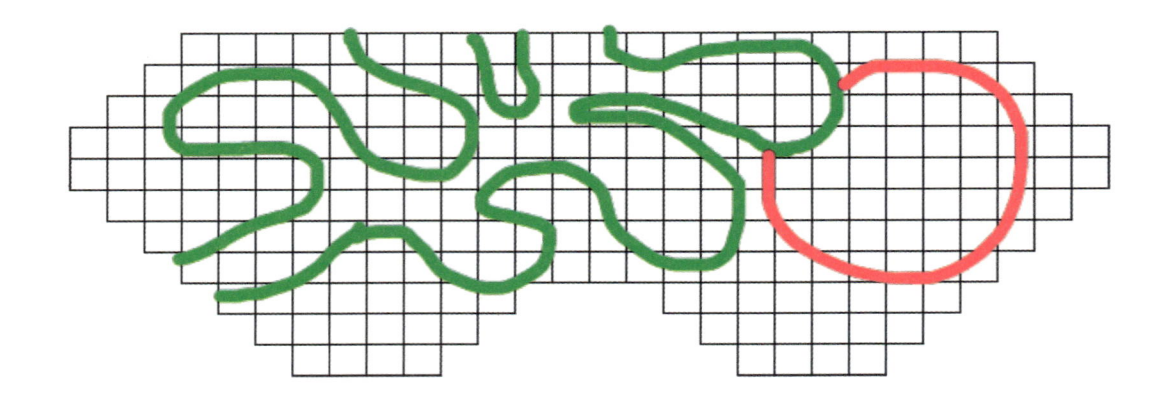

Surface crochet

Using Yarn B and one eye mask base, RS facing, surface crochet the leaf design as shown.
Using Yarn C on the same eye mask base, surface crochet the circle design as shown. Don't worry if your lines don't match exactly – Matisse was all about fluid lines!

Step 1 Insert hook from front to back of work in between two stitches, and yarn over on the back of the work, pull through to the front of the work, one loop on hook. **(Fig. 1)**

Step 2 Insert hook from front to back of the work, coming down in between next two stitches, or next row up/down, depending on the direction you want to move in. Yarn over on the back of the work, pull through to the front of the work, two loops on hook.

Step 3 Make a slip stitch on the front of the work by pulling the second loop formed through the first loop. The slip stitch will sit on the top of the work and look like the top of a chain. **(Fig. 2)**

Step 4 Repeat steps 2-3, moving around the eye mask base to create the pattern shown. **(Fig. 3)**

Step 5 To fasten off, cut the yarn behind the work, leaving a 10cm tail. Insert hook from front to back, yarn over, and pull tail up all the way through to the front of the piece, and ss to pull through the loop on the hook. Using a yarn needle, thread the tail and sew down from front to back, just off to the side of where you just came up, then sew the tail end to the back of the piece to secure it.

CHAPTER TWO: MATISSE EYE MASK

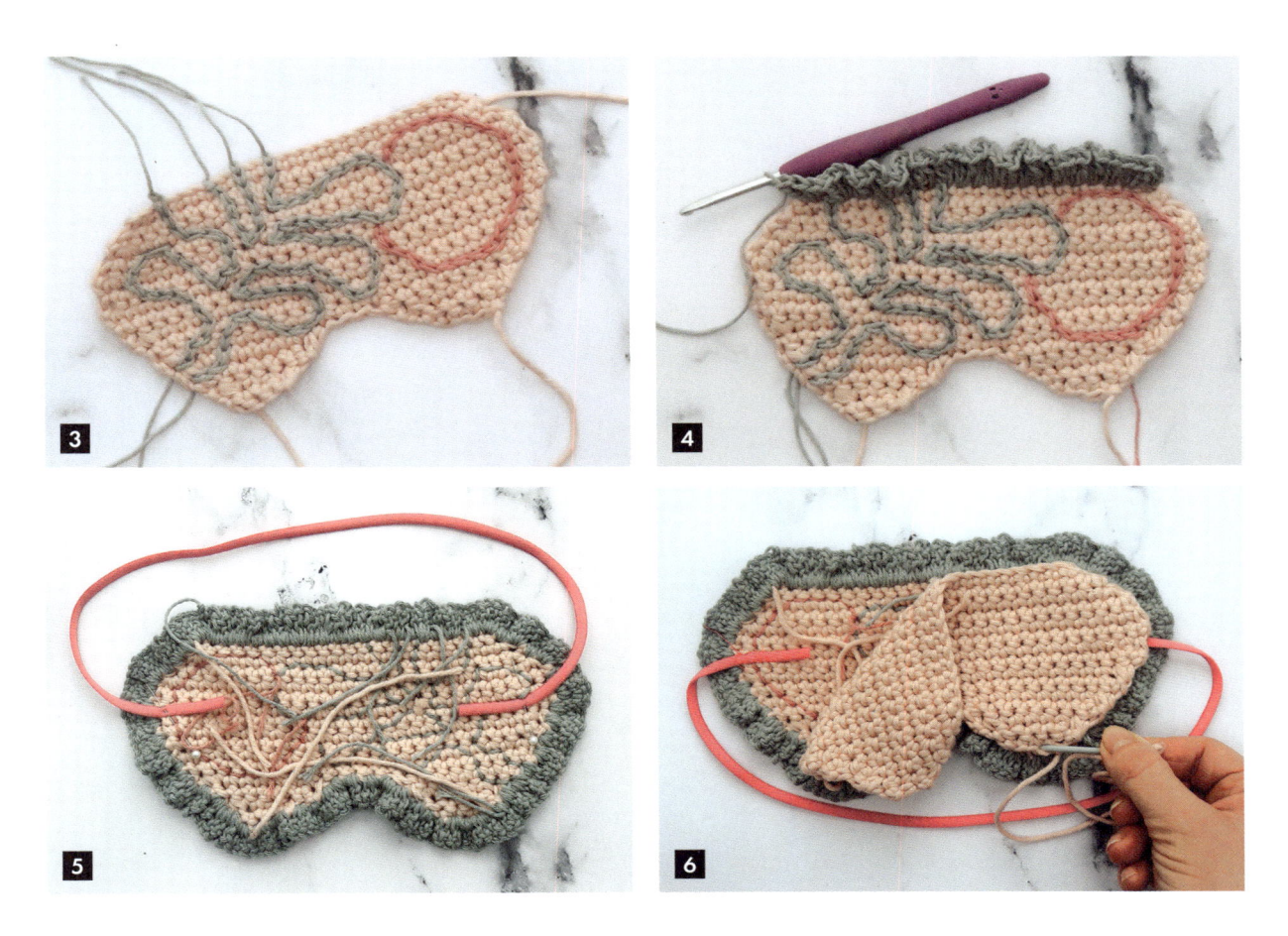

Frill Edge

Using Yarn B, attach to the first ch in row 1 with RS facing, and ch3 (counts as 1tr). Work 2tr in the base of the same stitch. Working around the outside of the eye mask, work 3tr in each stitch. When you reach the sides, work 3tr into the side of each row. Continue until you reach the first ch3, ss into the top of the ch, cut yarn and fasten off with a ss. **(Fig. 4)**

MAKING UP

Step 1 Cut a piece of covered elastic approx. 50cm long, and pin both ends to the inside of the eye mask, in the middle, and overlapping by about 2cm. Carefully check that this tension is correct for your head, before sewing the elastic to the back of the eye mask. Catch the back of the stitches and the sides of the elastic, but don't sew straight through to the front of the mask. **(Fig. 5)**

Step 2 With the elastic sewn firmly in place and the pins removed, place the second eye mask panel over the back of the eye mask, covering up your ends and the elastic ends. Using a yarn needle and a long length of Yarn A, sew the back panel to the front, by stitching evenly around from the back right through to the front. Come up and down in the same stitches you worked the frill border into, working inside the frill border. **(Fig. 6)**

Step 3 Sew in any ends that you weren't able to encase in the two layers of facemask. Your mask is now ready to wear. Happy snoozing!

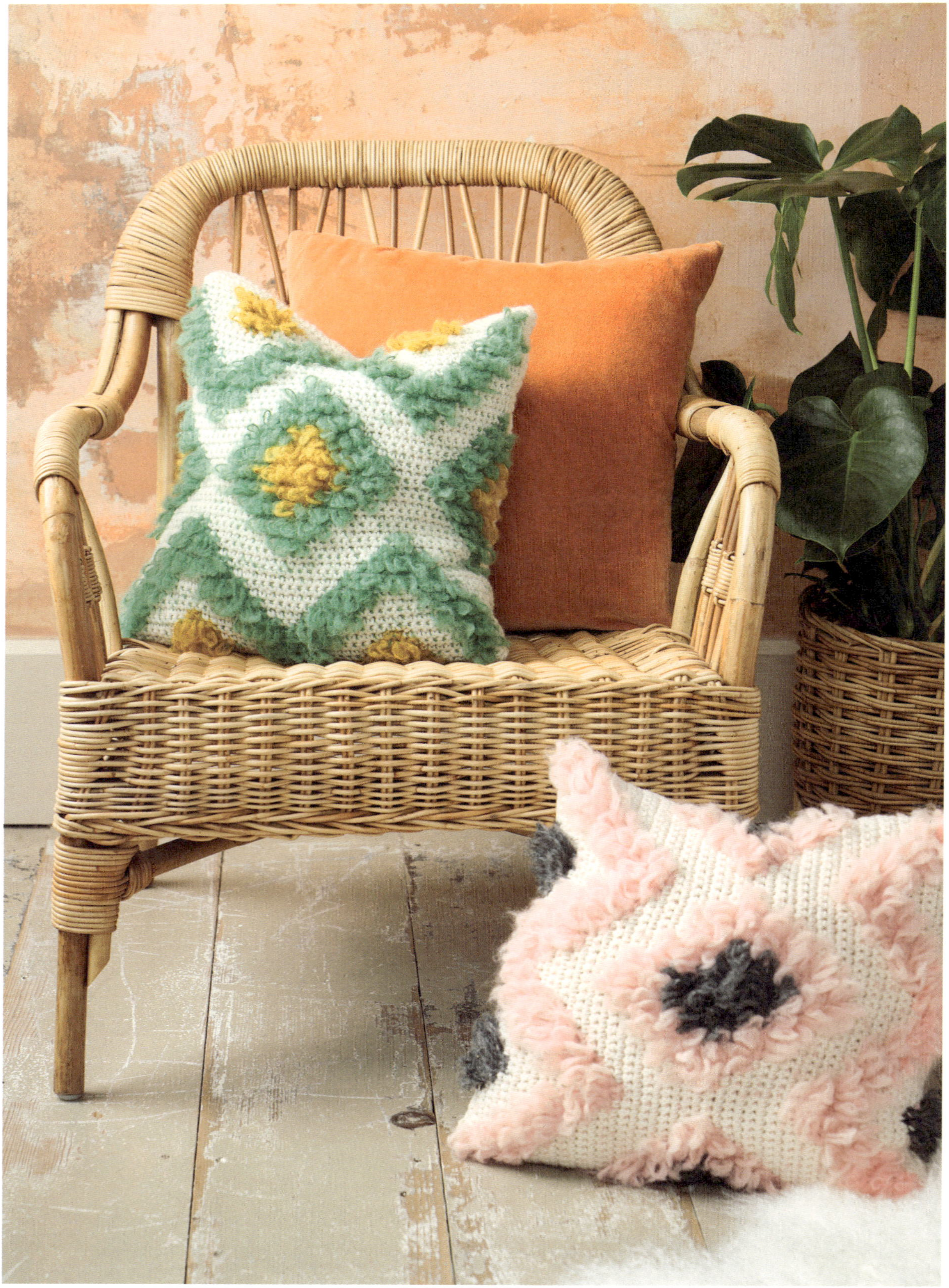

loopy cushion

Inspired by hand-woven North African carpets, this loopy cushion is all about texture and the depth of the loop stitch. Worked flat in rows, the cushion back features a handy envelope close design to easily remove the cushion pad.

You will need
- Rico Fashion Alpaca Dream, 50g/120m/131yd, 64% Virgin Wool/30% Alpaca/6% Polyamide
  Yarn A Cream (001) x 2 balls
  Rico Fashion Light Luxury, 50g/130m/142yd, 74% Alpaca/22% Wool/4% Nylon
  Yarn B Green (031) x 1 ball (or Anthracite (029) for second colourway)
  Yarn C Mustard (030) x 1 ball (or Powder (009) for second colourway)
- 7mm crochet hook
- 40cm x 40cm cushion pad

Yarn profile
The yarn is a light bouclé, but if loop stitch isn't your bag you can follow the pattern using only double crochet stitches so the yarn creates the texture.

Finished size
40cm x 40cm

Techniques – see p.12
Crochet Colourwork, Intarsia Crochet, Loop Stitch, Tapestry Crochet

Gauge
10cm x 10cm = 13sts x 14rows, worked in dc with Yarn A and carrying Yarn B

LINDSEY'S TIPS

- This pattern uses tapestry crochet for the main colours Yarn A and Yarn B, where the unworked yarn is carried. But the small pops of Yarn C use intarsia crochet, see Techniques p.12.
- Written instructions are provided overleaf, but you may find it easier to follow the chart once you get going.
- Starting chains do not count as stitches throughout.
- Where the pattern reads 7dcB – this should be read as 7 double crochet in Yarn B, and so on.

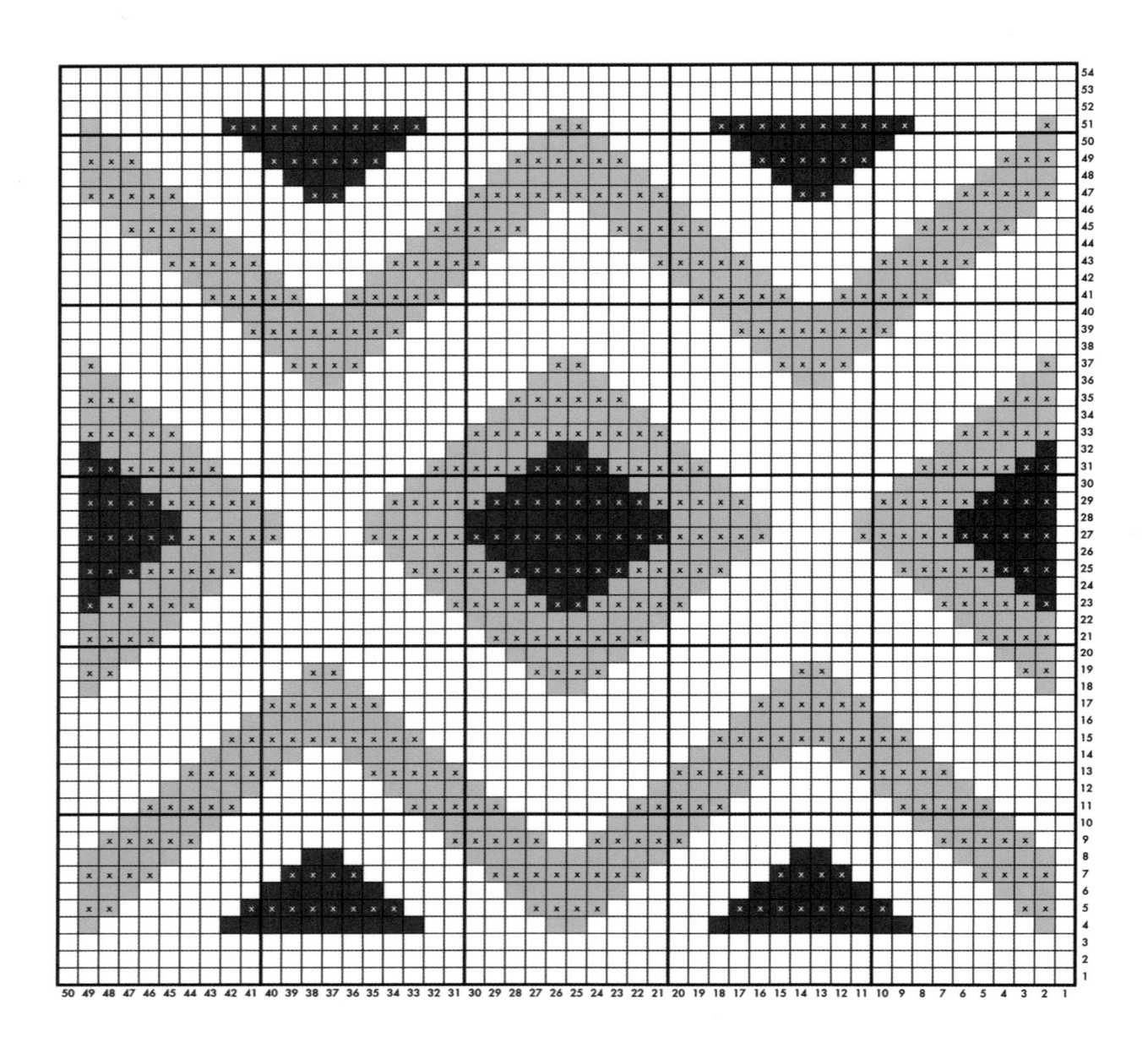

MODERN CROCHET STYLE

KEY

Yarn A ☐
Yarn B ▨
Yarn C ■
Loop stitch x

CHART

The chart is read from the bottom right to left for Row 1, left to right for Row 2, right to left for Row 3, and so on, alternating direction for every row. Each square on the chart represents a double crochet stitch. Each square on the chart marked with an X represents a loop stitch.

52

CHAPTER TWO: LOOPY CUSHION

PATTERN
Front panel – make 1
Wind three small balls of Yarn C off from the main ball, ready for the intarsia sections. **(Fig. 1)**
F using Yarn A, ch51.
Bring in Yarn B and carry throughout, tapestry crochet style.
Row 1 starting in 2nd ch from hook, 50dcA, turn. (50sts)
Rows 2-3 ch1, 50dcA, turn.
Row 4 1dcA, *1dcB, 6dcA, bring in 1 ball of Yarn C intarsia style 10dcC, 6dcA, 1dcB; rep from * until 1ch remains, 1dcA, turn.
Row 5 ch1, 1dcA, *2lsB, 6dcA, 8lsC, 6dcA, 2lsB; rep from * until 1st remains, 1dcA, turn.
Row 6 ch1, 1dcA, *3dcB, 6dcA, 6dcC, 6dcA, 3dcB; rep from * until 1st remains, 1dcA, turn.
Row 7 ch1, 1dcA, *4lsB, 6dcA, 4lsC, 6dcA, 4lsB; rep from * until 1st remains, 1dcA, turn.
Row 8 ch1, 1dcA, *5dcB, 6dcA, 2dcC, 6dcA, 5dcB; rep from * until 1st remains, 1dcA, turn. Cut and weave in Yarn C ends on two intarsia sections.
Row 9 ch1, 2dcA, *5lsB, 12dcA, 5lsB, 2dcA; rep from * until end, turn.
Row 10 ch1, 3dcA, 5dcB, 10dcA, 5dcB, 4dcA, 5dcB, 10dcA, 5dcB, 3dcA, turn.
Row 11 ch1, 4dcA, 5lsB, 8dcA, 5lsB, 6dcA, 5lsB, 8dcA, 5lsB, 4dcA, turn.
Row 12 ch1, 5dcA, 5dcB, 6dcA, 5dcB, 8dcA, 5dcB, 6dcA, 5dcB, 5dcA, turn.
Row 13 ch1, 6dcA, 5lsB, 4dcA, 5lsB, 10dcA, 5lsB, 4dcA, 5lsB, 6dcA, turn.
Row 14 ch1, 7dcA, 5dcB, 2dcA, 5dcB, 12dcA, 5dcB, 2dcA, 5dcB, 7dcA, turn.
Row 15 ch1, 8dcA, 10lsB, 14dcA, 10lsB, 8dcA, turn.
Row 16 ch1, 9dcA, 8dcB, 16dcA, 8dcB, 9dcA, turn.
Row 17 ch1, 10dcA, 6lsB, 18dcA, 6lsB, 10dcA, turn.
Row 18 ch1, 1dcA, *1dcB, 9dcA, 4dcB, 9dcA, 1dcB; rep from * until 1st remains, 1dcA, turn.
Row 19 ch1, 1dcA, *2lsB, 9dcA, 2lsB, 9dcA, 2lsB; rep from * until 1st remains, 1dcA, turn.
Row 20 ch1, 1dcA, *3dcB, 18dcA, 3dcB; rep from * until 1st remains, 1dcA, turn.
Row 21 ch1, 1dcA, *4lsB, 16dcA, 4lsB; rep from * until 1st remains, 1dcA, turn.
Row 22 ch1, 1dcA, *5dcB, 14dcA, 5dcB; rep from * until 1st remains, 1dcA, turn.
Row 23 ch1, 1dcA, bring in 1 ball of Yarn C intarsia style 1lsC, 5lsB, 12dcA, 5lsB, bring in 1 ball of Yarn C intarsia style 2lsC, 5lsB, 12dcA, 5lsB, bring in 1 ball of Yarn C intarsia style 1lsC, 1dcA, turn.
Row 24 ch1, 1dcA, *2dcC, 5dcB, 10dcA, 5dcB, 2dcC; rep from * until 1st remains, 1dcA, turn.
Row 25 ch1, 1dcA, *3lsC, 5lsB, 8dcA, 5lsB, 3lsC; rep from * until 1st remains, 1dcA, turn.
Row 26 ch1, 1dcA, *4dcC, 5dcB, 6dcA, 5dcB, 4dcA; rep from * until 1st remains, 1dcA, turn.
Row 27 ch1, 1dcA, *5lsC, 5lsB, 4dcA, 5lsB, 5lsC; rep from * until 1st remains, 1dcA, turn.
Row 28 ch1, 1dcA, *5dcC, 5dcB, 4dcA, 5dcB, 5dcC; rep from * until 1st remains, 1dcA, turn.
Row 29 ch1, 1dcA, *4lsC, 5lsB, 6dcA, 5lsB, 4dcA; rep from * until 1st remains, 1dcA, turn.

Row 30 ch1, 1dcA, *3dcC, 5dcB, 8dcA, 5dcB, 3dcC; rep from * until 1st remains, 1dcA, turn.
Row 31 ch1, 1dcA, *2lsC, 5lsB, 10dcA, 5lsB, 2lsC; rep from * until 1st remains, 1dcA, turn.
Row 32 ch1, 1dcA, 1dcC, 5dcB, 12dcA, 5dcB, 2dcC, 5dcB, 12dcA, 5dcB, 1dcC, 1dcA, turn. Cut and weave in Yarn C ends on three intarsia sections. **(Fig. 2&3)**
Row 33 ch1, 1dcA, *5lsB, 14dcA, 5lsB; rep from * until 1st remains, 1dcA, turn.
Row 34 ch1, 1dcA, *4dcB, 16dcA, 4dcB; rep from * until 1st remains, 1dcA, turn.
Row 35 ch1, 1dcA, *3lsB, 18dcA, 3lsB; rep from * until 1st remains, 1dcA, turn.
Row 36 ch1, 1dcA, *2dcB, 9dcA, 2dcB, 9dcA, 2dcB; rep from * until 1st remains, 1dcA, turn.
Row 37 ch1, 1dcA, *1lsB, 9dcA, 4lsB, 9dcA, 1lsB; rep from * until 1st remains, 1dcA, turn.
Row 38 ch1, 10dcA, 6dcB, 18dcA, 6dcB, 10dcA, turn.
Row 39 ch1, 9dcA, 8lsB, 16dcA, 8lsB, 9dcA, turn.
Row 40 ch1, 8dcA, 10dcB, 14dcA, 10dcB, 8dcA, turn.

Row 41 ch1, 7dcA, 5lsB, 2dcA, 5lsB, 12dcA, 5lsB, 2dcA, 5lsB, 7dcA, turn.
Row 42 ch1, 6dcA, 5dcB, 4dcA, 5dcB, 10dcA, 5dcB, 4dcA, 5dcB, 6dcA, turn.
Row 43 ch1, 5dcA, 5lsB, 6dcA, 5lsB, 8dcA, 5lsB, 6dcA, 5lsB, 5dcA, turn.
Row 44 ch1, 4dcA, 5dcB, 8dcA, 5dcB, 6dcA, 5dcB, 8dcA, 5dcB, 4dcA, turn.
Row 45 ch1, 3dcA, 5lsB, 10dcA, 5lsB, 4dcA, 5lsB, 10dcA, 5lsB, 3dcA, turn.
Row 46 ch1, 2dcA, *5dcB, 12dcA, 5dcB, 2dcA; rep from * until end, turn.
Row 47 ch1, 1dcA, *5lsB, 6dcA, bring in 1 ball of Yarn C intarsia style 2lsC, 6dcA, 5lsB; rep from * until 1st remains, 1dcA, turn.
Row 48 ch1, 1dcA, *4dcB, 6dcA, 4dcC, 6dcA, 4dcB; rep from * until 1st remains, 1dcA, turn.
Row 49 ch1, 1dcA, *3lsB, 6dcA, 6lsC, 6dcA, 3lsB; rep from * until 1st remains, 1dcA, turn.
Row 50 ch1, 1dcA, *2dcB, 6dcA, 8dcC, 6dcA, 2dcB; rep from * until 1st remains, 1dcA, turn.
Row 51 1dcA, *1lsB, 6dcA, 10lsC, 6dcA, 1lsB; rep

CHAPTER TWO: LOOPY CUSHION

from * until 1ch remains, 1dcA, turn. Cut and weave in Yarn C ends on two intarsia sections.
Rows 52-54 ch1, 50dcA, turn. Cut and weave in Yarn B end.

With Yarn A still attached, work a line of double crochet stitches down each of the sides of the front panel as follows: ch1, work 54dc evenly into the sides of the rows down the side of the cushion, cut yarn and fasten off with a ss. Repeat for the opposite side of the panel. Cut yarn and fasten off with a ss. Weave in Yarn A ends. **(Fig. 4)**

Back panel – make 2
F using Yarn A, ch51.
Bring in a second strand of Yarn A and carry throughout, tapestry crochet style.
Row 1 starting in 2nd ch from hook, 50dcA, turn. (50sts)
Rows 2-36 ch1, 50dcA, turn.
Cut both strands of Yarn A and fasten off working yarn with a ss. Weave in ends.

MAKING UP
Step 1 Lay your front panel right side up, and ensure no loops overlap the outside edge of the panel. Lay the two back panels on top, with the top and bottom of the back panels level with the top and bottom of the front panel. The two back panels will overlap in the middle, envelope-style. **(Fig. 5)**
Step 2 Attach Yarn A to one of the corners and chain one. Work evenly in each of the outside dc of the front panel, crocheting through two panels. Where all three panels overlap you will need to crochet though three layers. At each corner ch2. **(Fig. 6)**
Cut yarn A and fasten off with a ss, weave in ends.
Step 3 Turn cushion right side out and insert your cushion pad to complete. **(Fig. 7)**

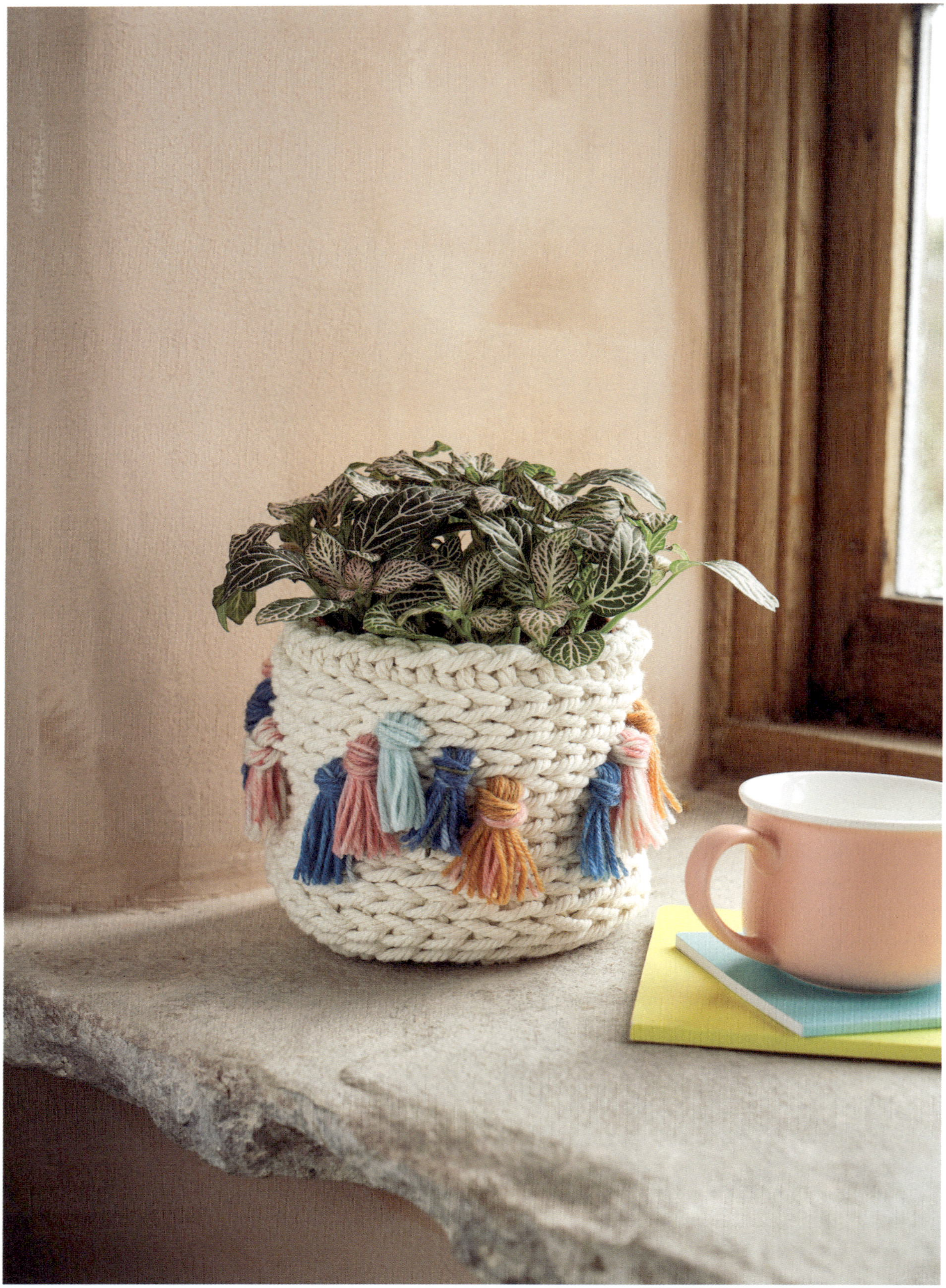

tassel basket

This little project is deceptively simple. The basket is all created in double crochet, but the stitch is worked into the back bump only, creating a textured chain effect on the outside of the basket. Plus, the tassels are made from just one ball of yarn. Clever, eh? These tassels are also a perfect way to use up scraps.

You will need
- Woolly Mahoosive 5mm Macrame and Crochet Cord, 100m roll, 100% recycled cotton, 4ply twisted
  Yarn A Cream x 1 roll
- Adriafil Knitcol, 50g/125m/137yd, 100% Merino Wool, DK weight
  Yarn B Klimt (70) x 1 ball
- 9mm crochet hook
- Stitch marker

Yarn profile
Chunky cotton cord just calls out to be made into baskets. It gives great structure and durability, and the neutral colours suit any home décor.

Finished size
H 14cm x D 15cm

Techniques – see p.12
Back Bump Only
Back Loop Only
Magic Loop
Working in the Round – Spiral Method

Gauge
Not essential

LINDSEY'S TIPS
- Work your stitches on the body of the basket a little looser than normal, to compensate for the cotton cord and the tightness of the back bump-only stitches.
- To keep your place while working in the round in a spiral, use a stitch marker to mark the last stitch of each round.

PATTERN
Basket
F Using Yarn A, ML and ch1.
Rnd 1 6dc into ML and pull closed. (6sts)
Rnd 2 dcinc in each st around. (12sts)

Rnd 3 *1dc, dcinc; rep from * 5 more times. (18sts)
Rnd 4 *2dc, dcinc; rep from * 5 more times. (24sts)
Rnd 5 *3dc, dcinc; rep from * 5 more times. (30sts)
(Fig. 1, previous page)
Rnd 6 30dc BLO.
(Fig. 2) Rnds 7-15 30dc BBO.
(Fig. 3&4) Fasten off yarn with a ss, cut and weave in ends.

Tassels

Using Yarn B, wrap around your hand or an 8cm piece of card until you reach a colour change. If using DK weight scrap yarn, wrap around 6 times. Cut the loops so you have a set of threads of equal length and fold each set in half to form a tassel. Repeat 20 times. **(Fig. 5)**

CHAPTER TWO: TASSEL BASKET

MAKING UP
Attach 4 tassels to Rnd 13 of the basket, 6-7 stitches apart using a lark's head knot.
Step 1 Insert hook in stitch from underneath through the back loop (top loop) of the stitch. Hook the middle of the tassel and pull down through the stitch, till the tassel sits halfway through. **(Fig. 6&7)**
Step 2 Take hold of the tail ends of the tassel, and pull these down and through the folded top of the tassel. Pull to tighten. **(Fig. 8)**
Step 3 Attach 2 more tassels to the stitches one round below, and one stitch to the left and right of the first tassels.
Step 4 Repeat this process once more, until all 20 tassels are attached, forming 4 inverted V shapes.
Step 5 Finally, trim tassels to shape using sharp scissors, to create a neat, flat base to each tassel. **(Fig. 9).** Your basket is done!

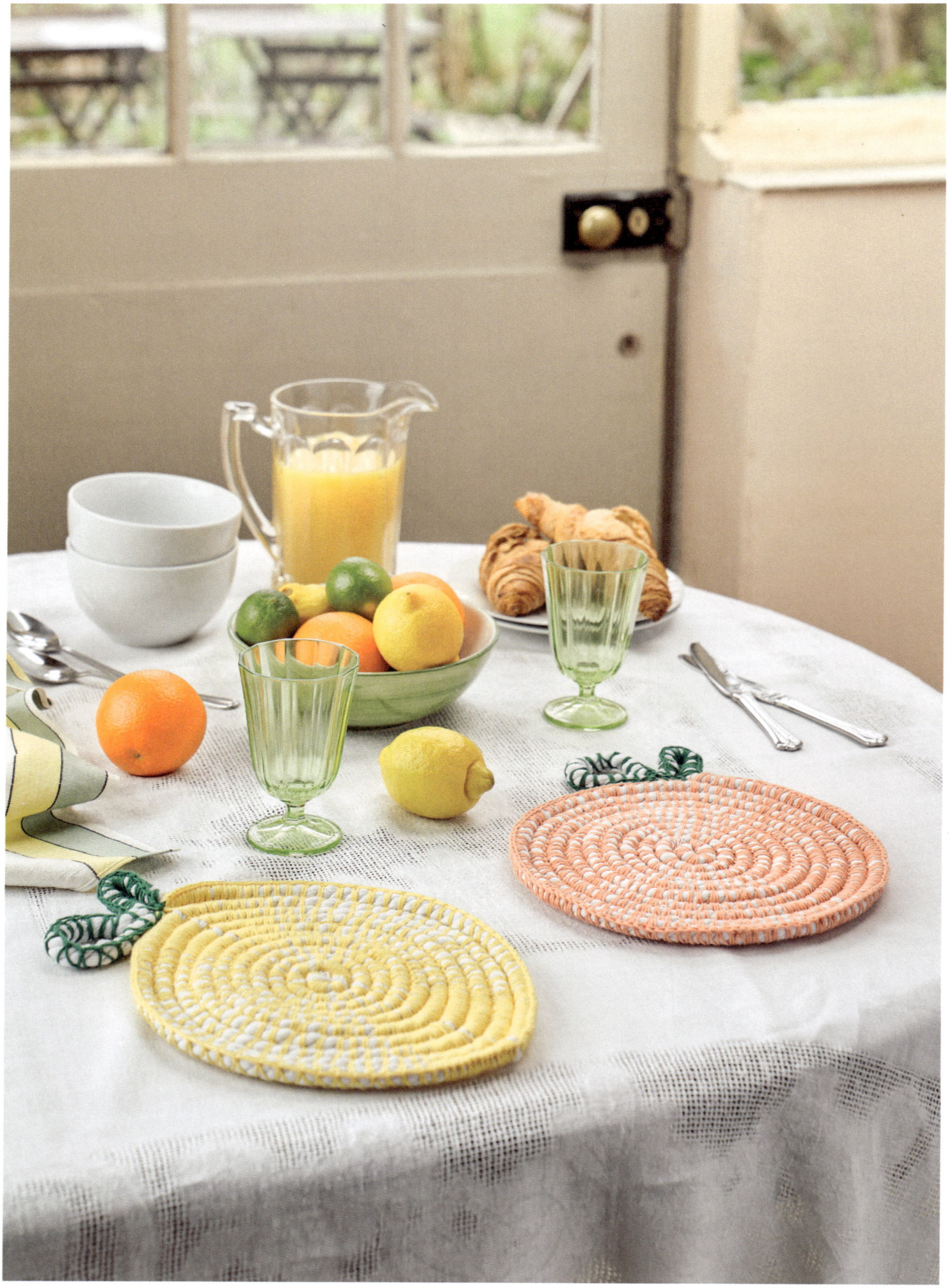

fruit placemats

Working with cord in crochet doesn't have to be hard on your hands – these fruit mats use just a 4mm hook and DK weight cotton. Pair your finished placemats with a gingham tablecloth, coloured vintage glassware and sparkling lemonade for dreamy summer dining.

You will need

- Rico Design Ricorumi DK, 25g/57m/62yd, 100% cotton
  Yarn A Smokey Orange (024) x 2 balls
  Yarn B Yellow (006) x 2 balls
  Yarn C Fir Green (050) x 1 ball
- Woolly Mahoosive 10mm Chunky Macrame Cord, 23m roll, 100% recycled cotton, White x 1 roll
- 4mm crochet hook
- Stitch marker

Yarn profile
The recycled cotton cord adds bulk and structure but is carried inside the project and never crocheted with, meaning the project grows quickly but is gentle on your hands. I'll take that.

Finished size
Approx. 25cm x 25cm

Techniques – see p.12
Magic Loop
Tapestry Crochet
Working in the Round – Spiral Method

Gauge
Not essential

LINDSEY'S TIPS

- The macrame cord is never crocheted with but carried, tapestry crochet style, throughout.

- The placemats are worked in the round in a continuous spiral. Use a stitch marker to mark the last stitch of every round and move it each round to help you keep your place.

- If your placemats start to curl, you are working your stitches too tightly. When you pull up a loop, exaggerate this action to make the loop longer than normal. It should reach up and over the cord, to sit comfortably on top.

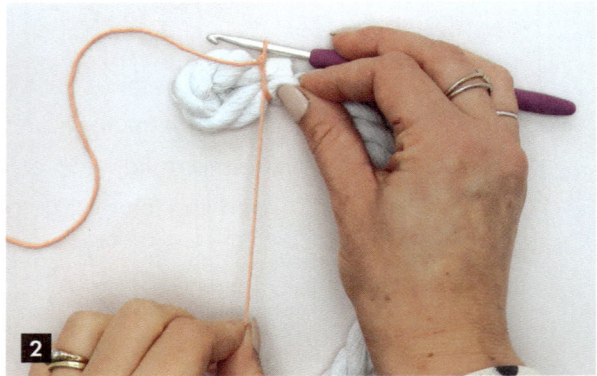

PATTERN

Peach

Using Yarn A, carrying cord.

F Create a ML and ch1. Take the end of your cord and fold the end over by 2-3cm to form a loop, with the end of the cord sitting on top. Insert the cord loop into your ML and pull to close. **(Fig. 1 & 2)**

Rnd 1 Working into the centre of the cord loop, 12dc evenly around the loop. (12sts) **(Fig. 3 & 4)**

Rnd 2 working into the prev rnd, carrying the cord as you go, *inc; rep from * 11 more times. (24sts)

Rnd 3 *1dc, dcinc; rep from * 11 more times. (36sts)

Rnd 4 *2dc, dcinc; rep from * 11 more times. (48sts)

Rnd 5 *3dc, dcinc; rep from * 11 more times. (60sts) **(Fig. 5)**

Rnd 6 *4dc, dcinc; rep from * 11 more times. (72sts)

Rnd 7 *5dc, dcinc; rep from * 11 more times. (84sts)

Rnd 8 *6dc, dcinc; rep from * 11 more times. (96sts)

Rnd 9 *7dc, dcinc; rep from * 11 more times. (108sts)

Rnd 10 *8dc, dcinc; rep from * 11 more times. (120sts)

On the last stitch of rnd 10, change colour to Yarn C. Cut and fasten off Yarn A by weaving in end.

Peach leaf

Using Yarn C only.

Step 1 moving the cord aside, ss into next dc from prev rnd, ch7.

Step 2 starting in 2nd ch from hook, 6dc back down ch, 1ss into the base of the same stitch as ch7. **(Fig. 6)**

Using Yarn C, carrying cord.

Step 3 make 5dc along the chain, dc3inc in top of chain, 5dc back down other side of ch. (13sts) **(Fig. 7)**

CHAPTER TWO: FRUIT PLACEMATS

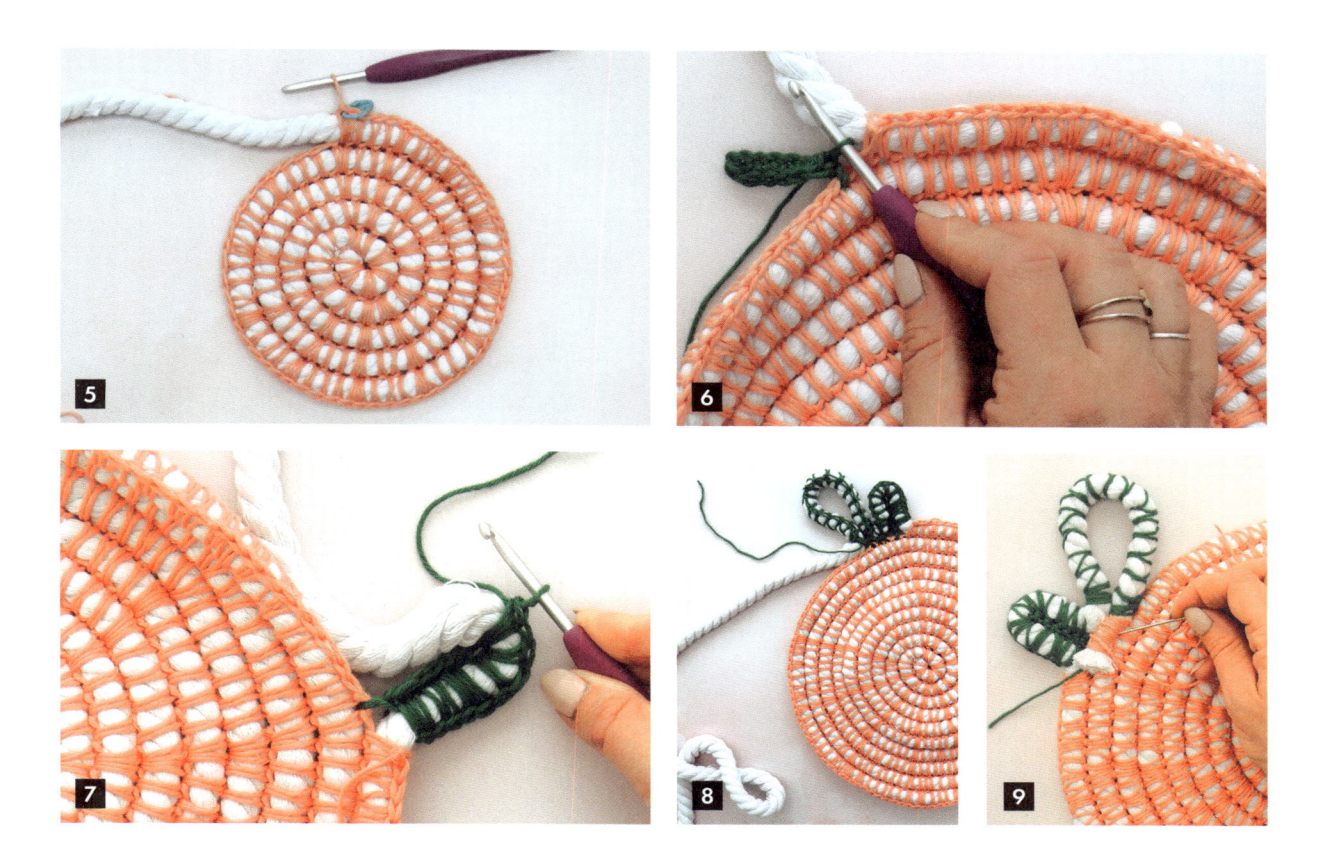

Step 4 2ss into next 2 unworked dc from prev Yarn A rnd.
Step 5 Crocheting over the top of the cord only, 16dc, ss into next unworked dc from prev Yarn A rnd.
Step 6 Cut and fasten off Yarn C using a ss, leave a 15cm tail. Cut the cord, leaving a 5cm tail. **(Fig. 8)**
Step 7 Turn the placemat over and use a yarn needle to sew over the top of the cord end 10-15 times, catching the stitches behind to anchor it down. Fasten off Yarn C and sew in all ends. **(Fig. 9)**

Lemon

Using Yarn B, carrying cord. Work as for Peach until end of Rnd 4.
Rnd 5 dc3inc, 18dc, dc3inc, ch2, dc3inc, 18dc, dc3inc, ch2. (60sts)
Rnd 6 dc3inc, 24dc, dc3inc, ch2 and sk ch2 from prev rnd, dc3inc, 24dc, dc3inc, ch2 and sk ch2 from prev rnd. (72sts)
Rnd 7 dc3inc, 30dc, dc3inc, ch2 and skip ch2 from prev rnd, dc3inc, 30dc, dc3inc, ch2 and skip ch2 from prev rnd. (84sts)
Rnd 8 dc3inc, 36dc, dc3inc, ch2 and skip ch2 from prev rnd, dc3inc, 36dc, dc3inc, ch2 and skip ch2 from prev rnd. (96sts)
Rnd 9 dc3inc, 42dc, dc3inc, ch2 and skip ch2 from prev rnd, dc3inc, 42dc, dc3inc, ch2 and skip ch2 from prev rnd. (108sts)
Rnd 10 dc3inc, 48dc, dc3inc, ch2 and skip ch2 from prev rnd, dc3inc, 48dc, dc3inc, ch2 and skip ch2 from prev rnd. (120sts)

Lemon leaf

Work as for Peach Leaf.

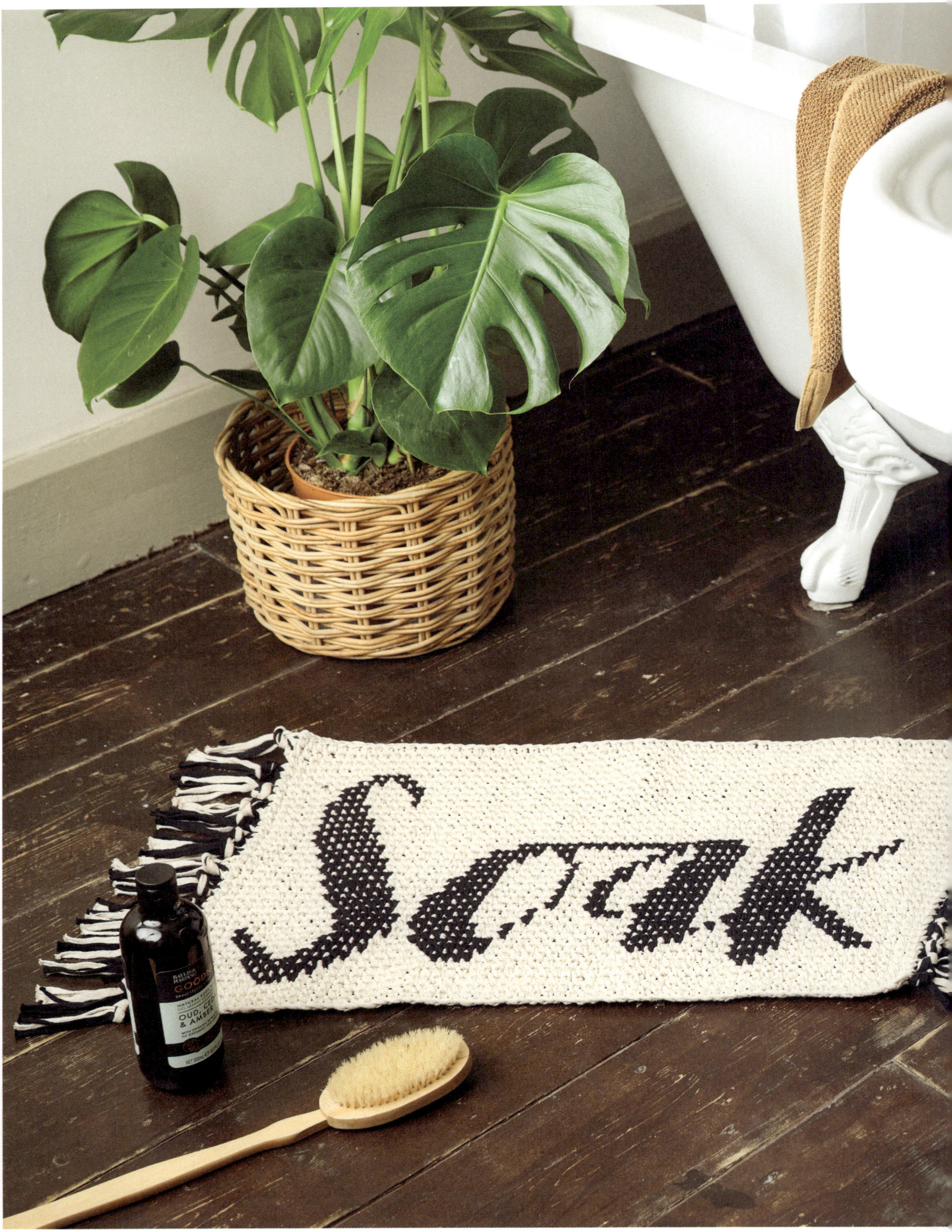
Soak

chapter three: autumn

Ahh, autumn, the yarn-lover's friend! As the weather turns cooler and the sun sinks lower, we can finally wrap up in our crochet makes. Hook up a patchwork-inspired scarf or take a leafy walk with your new pom pom duffel bag. Then in the evening, create that Hygge feeling with candles and a long soak in the tub... your slogan crochet bathmat will definitely put a smile on your face.

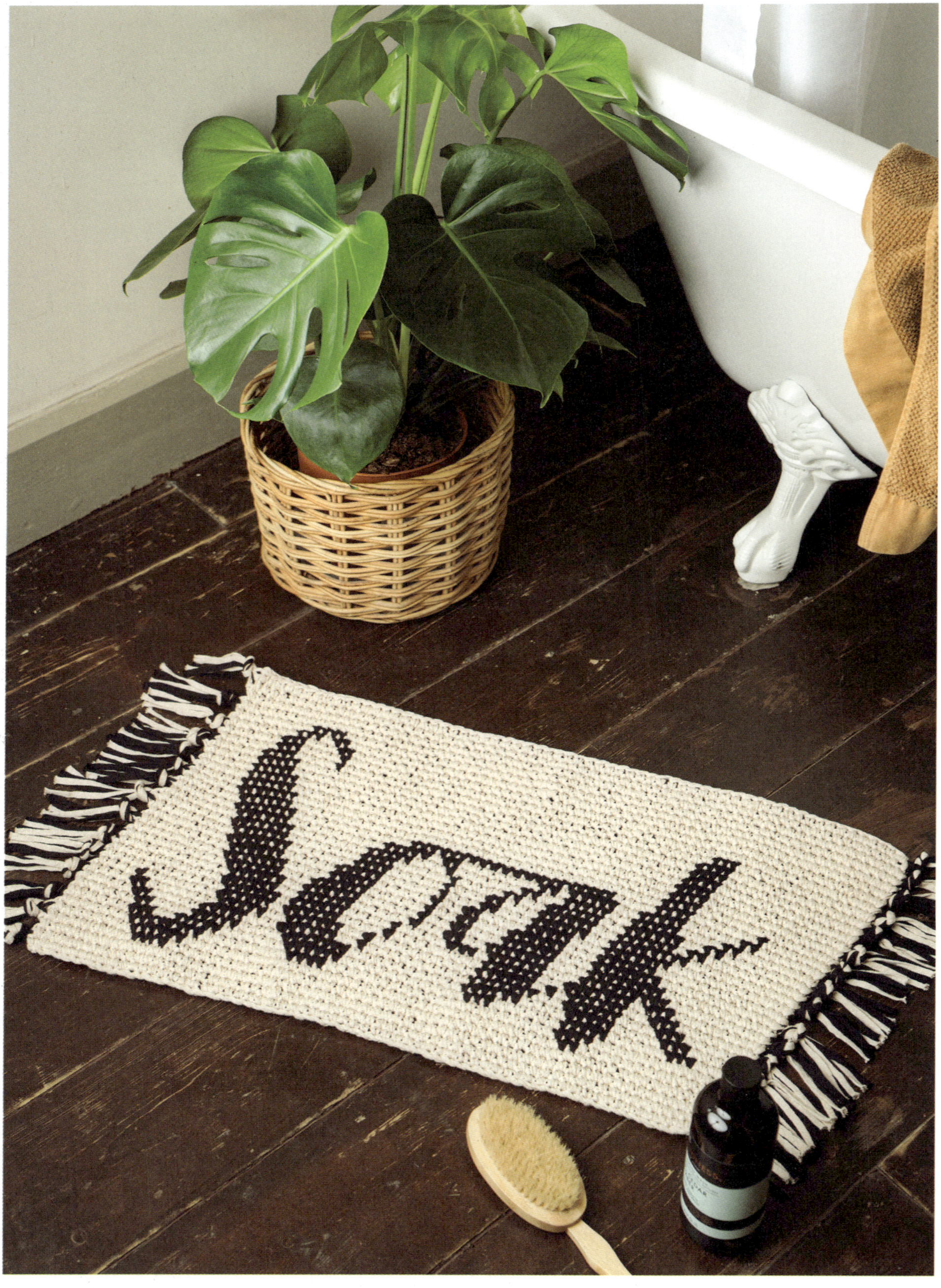
Soak

slogan bathmat

Your bathmat wants you to have a nice, long bath. Who are you to say no? This cute bathmat is worked flat in rows, with the yarns cut at the end of each row. This unusual construction allows us to add tassels (hello!) and to create the slogan in split double crochet, all on the front of the work.

You will need
- Wool and the Gang Mixtape Yarn, 250g/130m/142yd, 80% Cotton/20% Polyester
  Yarn A Sahara Dust x 2 rolls
  Yarn B Cinder Black x 1 roll
- 7mm crochet hook

Yarn profile
Made using t-shirt yarn, up-cycled from off-cuts in the textile industry, this Mixtape yarn is a feel-good fibre.

Finished size
W65cm x H40cm excluding tassels. The tassels add 20cm

Techniques – see p.12
Split Double Crochet Stitch
Standing Double Crochet
Tapestry Crochet

Gauge
10cm x 10cm = 9sts x 10 rows, worked in dc rows of Yarn A, carrying Yarn B

LINDSEY'S TIPS

- This project is a variation on tapestry crochet – the non-working yarn is carried in the same way, but the colour changes are slightly different due to the split double crochet stitch. See Techniques p.12.

- Your work will appear to slant slightly as you crochet – don't worry about this; it helps create the italic font.

- You will fasten off Yarn A at the end of each row, but Yarn B will be tied off in the Making Up section.

- Starting ch1 does not count as a stitch throughout.

- Where the pattern reads 7dcB – this should be read as 7 double crochet in Yarn B, and so on.

- Written instructions are provided overleaf, but you may find it easier to follow the chart once you get going.

MODERN CROCHET STYLE

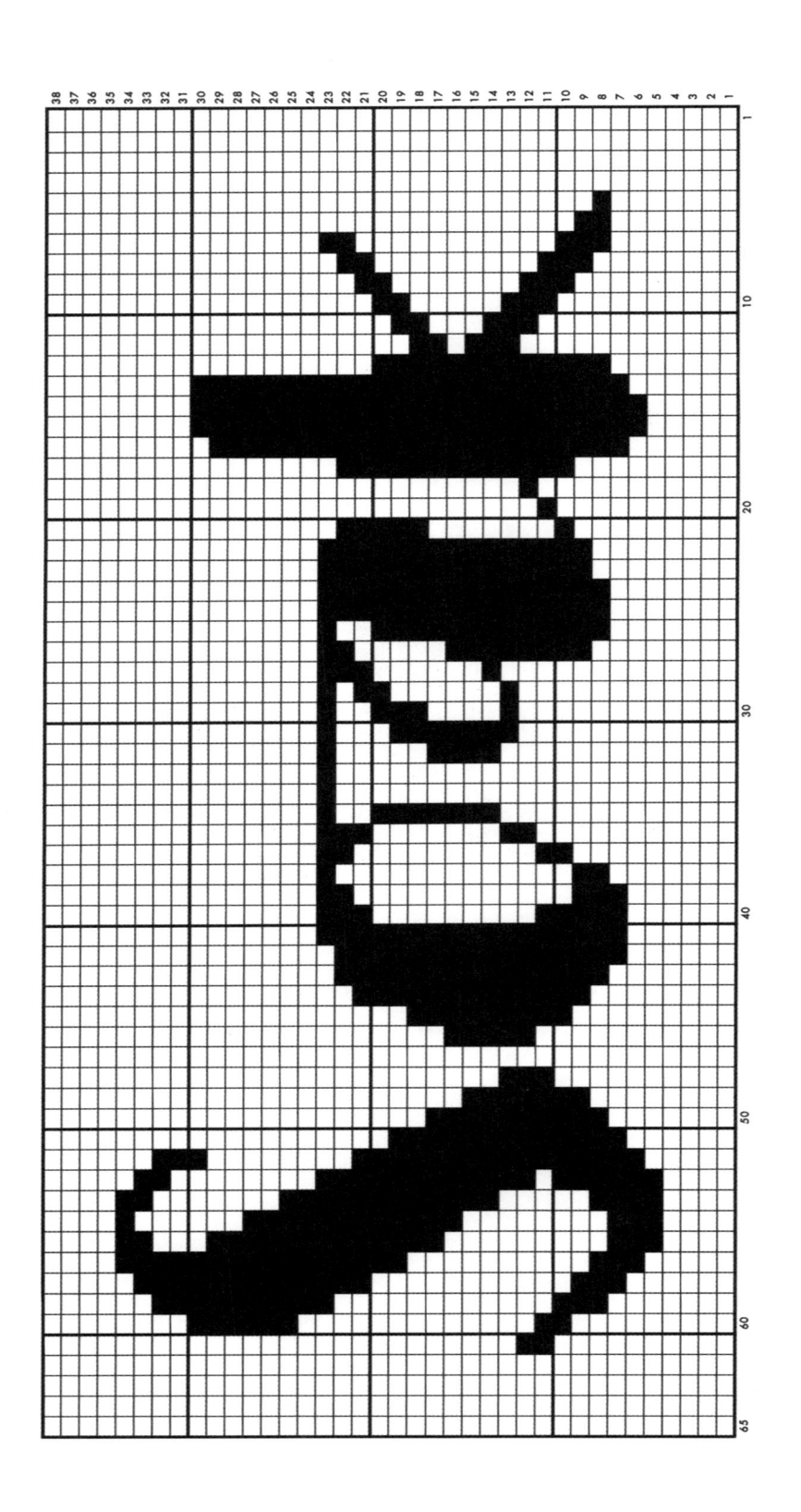

KEY
Split double crochet Yarn B ■
Double crochet Yarn A ☐

CHART
Read the chart from bottom right to left. You will start at the right side of the chart for every row. Each white square on the chart represents a double crochet stitch in Yarn A; each black square on the chart represents a split double crochet stitch in Yarn B.

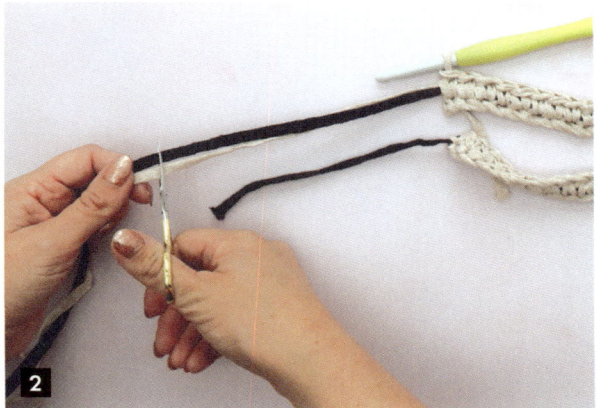

PATTERN

F using Yarn A, ch66.
Bring in Yarn B ready to carry and leave a tail end of 15cm in Yarn B overlapping the end of the row.
Row 1 Starting in the 2nd ch from the hook, 65dcA along ch. At the end of the row, cut both yarns with a 15cm long tail. Fasten off Yarn A with a ss. Do not turn work but return to the right-hand side of the work to reattach yarns. (65sts) **(Fig. 1 & 2)**

All future rows

Reattach Yarn A to the first dc of the previous row with a standing double crochet, leaving a 15cm long tail. Bring in Yarn B and place ready to carry, leaving a 15cm long tail. At the end of the row, cut both yarns with a 15cm long tail. Fasten off Yarn A. Do not turn. **(Fig. 3)**

Follow the chart using the split double crochet technique for each double crochet in Yarn B as explained OR use the written instructions below.
Row 2 ch1, 65dcA.
Rows 3-4 rep row 2.
Row 5 ch1, 52dcA, 4sdcB, 9dcA.
Row 6 ch1, 14dcA, 2sdcB, 35dcA, 6sdcB, 8dcA.
Row 7 ch1, 13dcA, 4sdcB, 21dcA, 4sdcB, 8dcA, 8sdcB, 7dcA.
Row 8 ch1, 4dcA, 3sdcB, 5dcA, 5sdcB, 6dcA, 3sdcB, 11dcA, 6sdcB, 6dcA, 5sdcB, 2dcA, 3sdcB, 6dcA.

Row 9 ch1, 5dcA, 3sdcB, 4dcA, 5sdcB, 4dcA, 6sdcB, 10dcA, 7sdcB, 4dcA, 5sdcB, 4dcA, 2sdcB, 6dcA.
Row 10 ch1, 6dcA, 3sdcB, 3dcA, 6sdcB, 2dcA, 7sdcB, 9dcA, 1sdcB, 2dcA, 6sdcB, 3dcA, 5sdcB, 5dcA, 2sdcB, 5dcA.
Row 11 ch1, 7dcA, 3sdcB, 2dcA, 6sdcB, 1dcA, 1sdcB, 1dcA, 6sdcB, 9dcA, 1sdcB, 2dcA, 6sdcB, 2dcA, 5sdcB, 7dcA, 2sdcB, 4dcA.
Row 12 ch1, 8dcA, 3sdcB, 1dcA, 7sdcB, 2dcA, 6sdcB, 8dcA, 1sdcB, 4dcA, 6sdcB, 1dcA, 6sdcB, 7dcA, 1sdcB, 4dcA.
Row 13 ch1, 9dcA, 9sdcB, 3dcA, 6sdcB, 1dcA, 3sdcB, 4dcA, 1sdcB, 4dcA, 6sdcB, 1dcA, 6sdcB, 12dcA.
Row 14 ch1, 10dcA, 8sdcB, 3dcA, 7sdcB, 2dcA, 2sdcB, 2dcA, 1sdcB, 5dcA, 6sdcB, 2dcA, 6sdcB, 11dcA.
Row 15 ch1, 11dcA, 7sdcB, 3dcA, 6sdcB, 3dcA, 2sdcB, 2dcA, 1sdcB, 5dcA, 6sdcB, 2dcA, 6sdcB, 11dcA.
Row 16 ch1, 12dcA, 6sdcB, 3dcA, 6sdcB, 3dcA, 2sdcB, 2dcA, 1sdcB, 5dcA, 6sdcB, 3dcA, 6sdcB, 10dcA.
Row 17 ch1, 11dcA, 7sdcB, 3dcA, 5sdcB, 4dcA, 2sdcB, 2dcA, 1sdcB, 5dcA, 5sdcB, 4dcA, 7sdcB, 9dcA. **(Fig. 4)**
Row 18 ch1, 10dcA, 8sdcB, 2dcA, 6sdcB, 3dcA, 2sdcB, 3dcA, 1sdcB, 5dcA, 5sdcB, 5dcA, 6sdcB, 9dcA.
Row 19 ch1, 9dcA, 2sdcB, 1dcA, 6sdcB, 2dcA, 6sdcB, 3dcA, 2sdcB, 3dcA, 1sdcB, 5dcA, 4sdcB,

6dcA, 7sdcB, 8dcA.
Row 20 ch1, 8dcA, 2sdcB, 2dcA, 6sdcB, 2dcA, 6sdcB, 2dcA, 2sdcB, 4dcA, 1sdcB, 5dcA, 4sdcB, 7dcA, 6sdcB, 8dcA.
Row 21 ch1, 7dcA, 2sdcB, 4dcA, 5sdcB, 2dcA, 5sdcB, 2dcA, 2sdcB, 6dcA, 1sdcB, 3dcA, 5sdcB, 7dcA, 7sdcB, 7dcA.
Row 22 ch1, 6dcA, 2sdcB, 5dcA, 5sdcB, 2dcA, 5sdcB, 1dcA, 2sdcB, 7dcA, 2sdcB, 1dcA, 5sdcB, 9dcA, 6sdcB, 7dcA.
Row 23 ch1, 6dcA, 1sdcB, 6dcA, 4sdcB, 4dcA, 20sdcB, 11dcA, 7sdcB, 6dcA.
Row 24 ch1, 13dcA, 4sdcB, 36dcA, 6sdcB, 6dcA.
Row 25 ch1, 13dcA, 4sdcB, 36dcA, 7sdcB, 5dcA.
Row 26 ch1, 13dcA, 4sdcB, 37dcA, 6sdcB, 5dcA.
Row 27 rep row 26.
Row 28 ch1, 13dcA, 4sdcB, 38dcA, 5sdcB, 5dcA.
Row 29 rep row 28.
Row 30 ch1, 13dcA, 3sdcB, 35dcA, 1sdcB, 4dcA, 4sdcB, 5dcA.
Row 31 ch1, 51dcA, 1sdcB, 4dcA, 3sdcB, 6dcA.
Row 32 ch1, 51dcA, 2sdcB, 3dcA, 3sdcB, 6dcA.
Row 33 ch1, 52dcA, 2sdcB, 1dcA, 3sdcB, 7dcA.
Row 34 ch1, 53dcA, 4sdcB, 8dcA.
Rows 35-38 rep row 2.
Fasten off and leave a final tail of 15cm for both A and B.

MAKING UP
Tie the ends on each side together in groups of 5 to form tassels, then trim each tassel to measure 10cm from the edge of the mat. **(Fig. 5 & 6)**

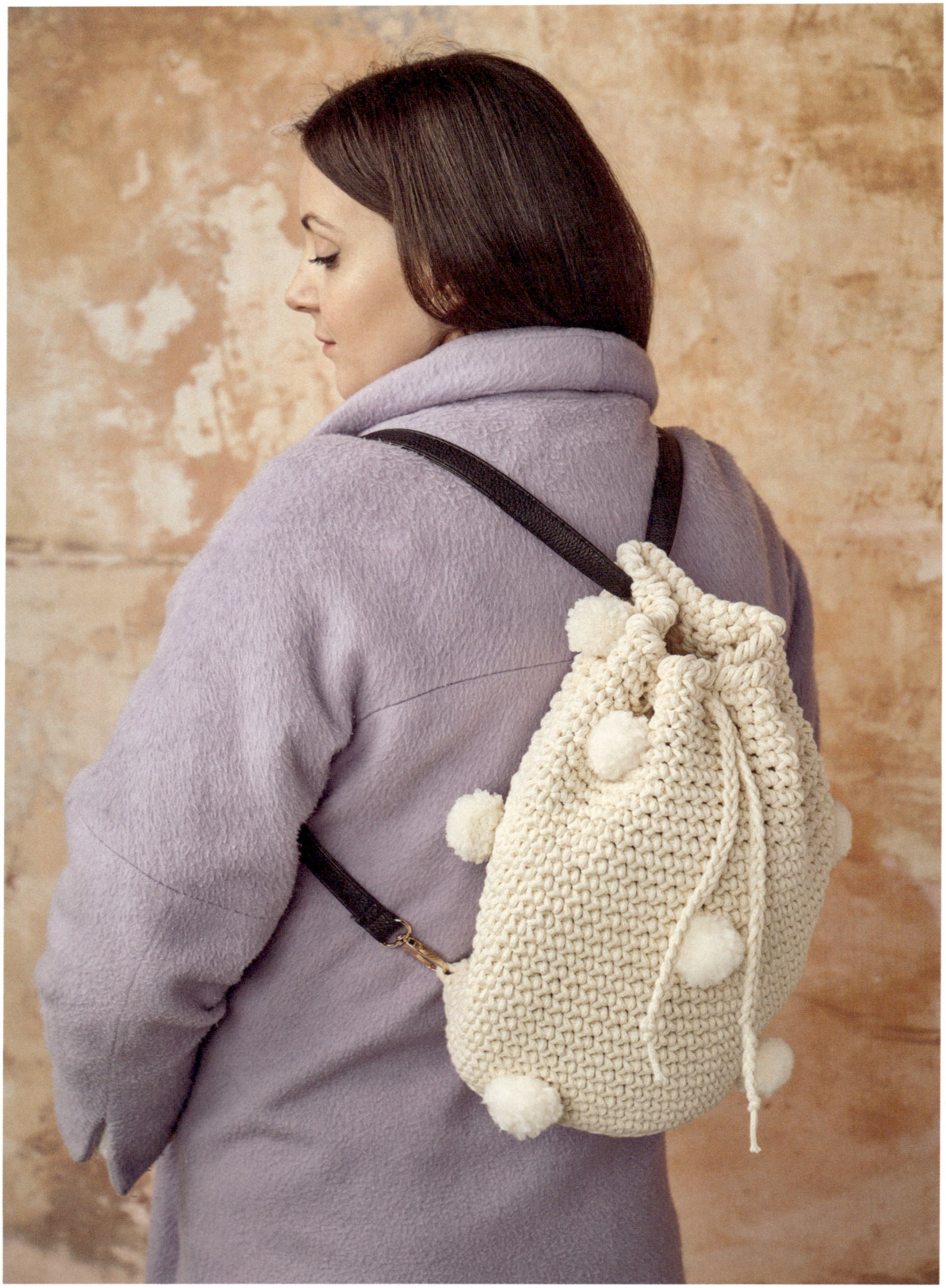

pom pom duffel bag

There is just something so satisfying about neat pom poms, isn't there? This backpack duffel bag is a really quick project to whip up over an evening or weekend. Then you just need to decide between fabric or yarn pom poms and add little bobbles of fun. It'll make you smile every time you use it.

You will need
- Knitcraft Return of the Mac Chunky Yarn, 100g/81m/89yd per ball, 100% Cotton, Ecru x 3 balls
- 8mm crochet hook
- Stitch marker
- Bag strap with clips (I used PU leather adjustable bag strap with clips, 2cm wide x 124cm long)
- 3.5cm pom pom maker
- 50cm x 50cm piece of fabric (I used Velboa animal print low-pile faux fur fabric, in Snow Leopard), strong cotton thread, sewing needle, toy stuffing (optional)

Yarn profile
This thick cotton cord is durable and hardwearing.

Finished size
H35cm x W30cm

Techniques – see p.12
Back Loop Only
Crab Stitch
Magic Loop
Working in the Round
 Spiral Method

Gauge
10cm x 10cm = 8.5sts x 10 rounds when worked in double crochet

LINDSEY'S TIPS

- An acrylic or animal fibre yarn will give you the best fluffy pom poms (avoid plant fibres as they tend to have less bounce and fluff).

- Use a stitch maker, or long tail end, at the end of each round to keep your place when working in the round – spiral method.

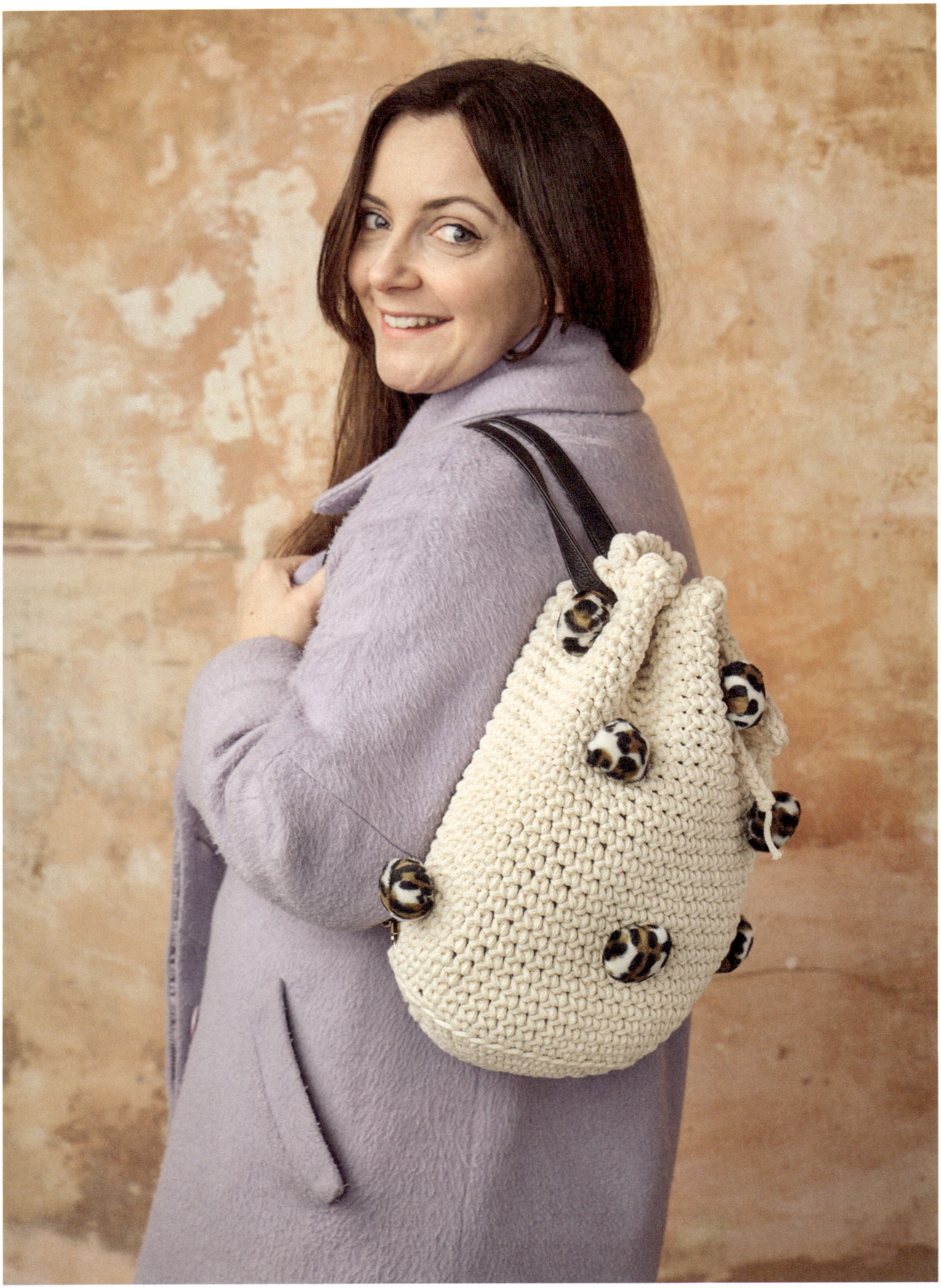

PATTERN

F ML, ch1.

Rnd 1 6dc into ML, pull ML tightly closed. PM into final stitch of the round. (6sts) **(Fig. 1)**

Rnd 2 dcinc 6 times. (12sts)

Rnd 3 *1dc, dcinc; rep from * 5 more times. (18sts)

Rnd 4 *2dc, dcinc; rep from * 5 more times. (24sts)

Rnd 5 *3dc, dcinc; rep from * 5 more times. (30sts)

Rnd 6 2dc, dcinc, *4dc, dcinc; rep from * 4 more times, 2dc. (36sts)

Rnd 7 *5dc, dcinc; rep from * 5 more times. (42sts)

Rnd 8 3dc, dcinc, *6dc, dcinc; rep from * 4 more times, 3dc. (48sts)

Rnd 9 *7dc, dcinc; rep from * 5 more times. (54sts) **(Fig. 2)**

Rnd 10 1dc BLO in each st around. (54sts) **(Fig. 3)**

Rnds 11-37 1dc in each st around. (54sts) **(Fig. 4 & 5)**

Rnd 38 *5dc, ch1 and sk1; rep from * 8 times. (54sts)

Rnd 39 dc in each st and ch-sp around. (54sts)

Rnd 40 cs in each st around. (54sts) **(Fig. 6)**

Fasten off and weave in any ends.

Yarn Pom Poms

Step 1 Use a 3.5cm pom pom maker and make 12 pom poms using scrap yarn in the same colour as your bag. **(Fig. 1)**

Step 2 Tie each pom pom with a piece of yarn approx. 30cm long, to give you enough length to tie the pom pom and then attach it to the bag.

Step 3 Attach to the bag by tying the ends over one stitch on the bag, in the pattern as shown in the pictures: 4 pom poms on rows 13, 24 and 35, spaced 15 stitches apart. **(Fig. 2)**

Fabric Pom Poms

Step 1 Draw 12 separate 9cm diameter circles on the reverse of your fabric, and cut them out.

Step 2 Sew a gathering stitch around the outside of each circle, about 5mm from the edge, using strong sewing cotton and a needle. Double up your thread and knot it at one end, then hand stitch a running stitch 5mm from the edge. Gently push the fabric towards the knotted end of the thread as you go. **(Fig. 1)**

Step 3 Place a small amount of toy stuffing or scrap

CHAPTER THREE: POM POM DUFFEL BAG

yarn ends in the centre of the circle, then pull your thread to close the pom pom. Sew the gathered fabric together with several strong stitches. **(Fig. 2)**
Step 3 Attach to the bag by sewing, as shown in the pictures: 4 pom poms on rows 13, 24 and 35, spaced 15 stitches apart. **(Fig. 3)**

Gathering Cord
To make the gathering cord, ch80, leaving a small tail at either end of the hook. Fasten off. **(Fig. 4)**

MAKING UP
Starting with one of the chain spaces from round 38 at the front of the bag, weave the gathering cord in and out of the chain spaces until you have two cords hanging down on the outside at the front of the bag in one chain space. **(Fig. 5)**
To attach your bag strap, weave it in and out of the two chain spaces at the back of the bag, then clip the ends to the bottom of the bag, through rows 10-11, spaced around 20cm apart. **(Fig. 6)**
Your bag is ready to use.

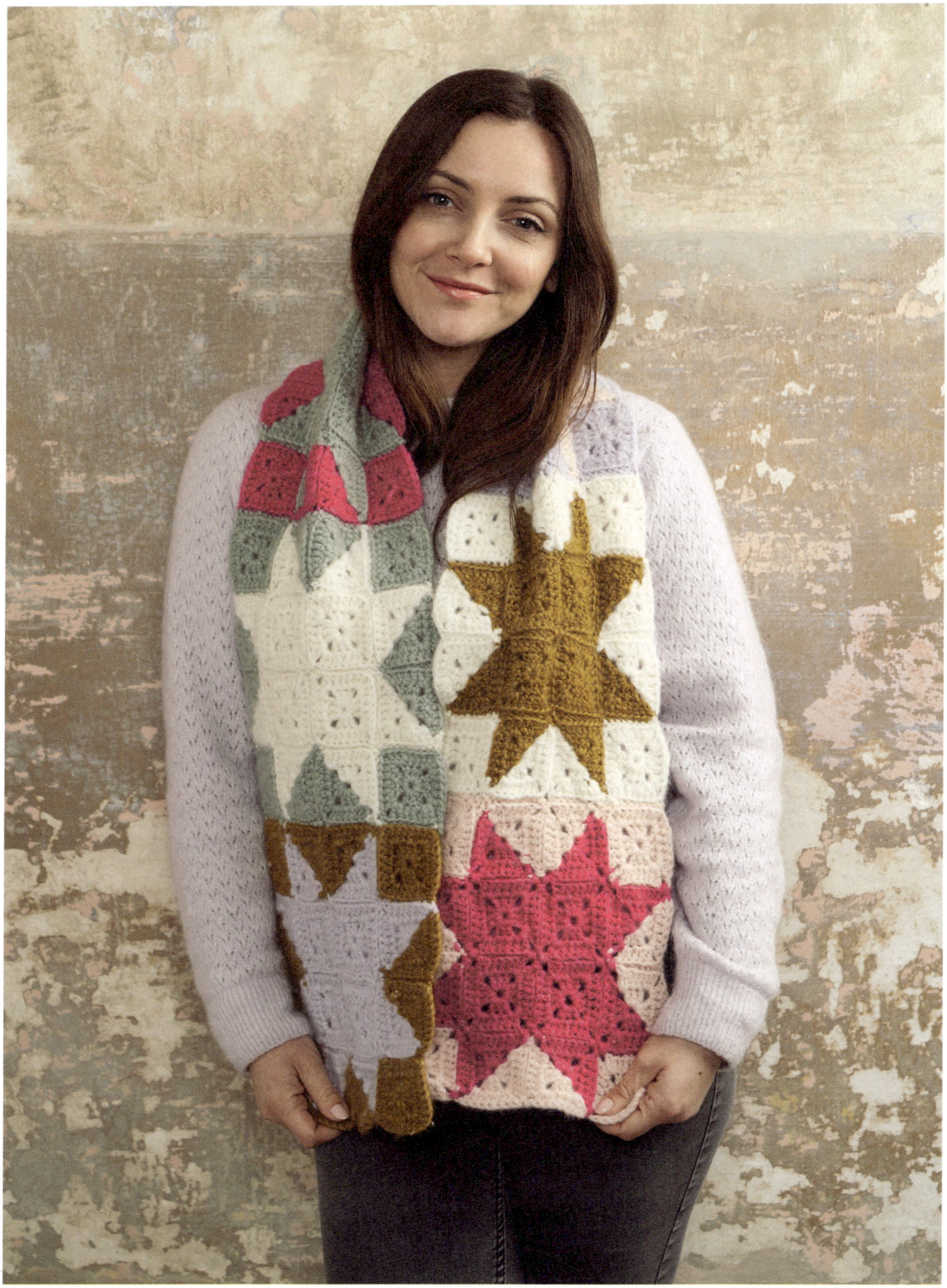

patchwork scarf

I can't tell you how happy it makes me to combine patchwork and crochet in this Eight-Point star block pattern. Growing up, my mum owned a patchwork shop and before I discovered crochet, sewing and patchwork were my jam! The half-square triangle is so clever. The number of patterns you can make from it is jaw dropping.

You will need
- Wool and the Gang Feeling Good Yarn, 50g/130m/142yd, 70% Baby Alpaca/23% Nylon/7% Merino Wool, Aran weight
  1 ball each in Ivory White, Cameo Rose, Hot Punk Pink, Lilac Powder, Bronzed Olive, Eucalyptus Green
- 5mm crochet hook

Yarn profile
The blend of fibres in this yarn make for a wonderful mix of warmth, strength and fluff. Better still, the mix of pastel and saturated colours makes this oversized patchwork design feel thoroughly modern.

Finished size
W25cm x L150cm

Techniques – see p.12
Crochet Colourwork
Working in the Round – Join Method

Gauge
1 half-square triangle made in pattern as described is 6cm x 6cm

LINDSEY'S TIPS

- Use 2 colours per Eight-Point Star block. For pattern purposes these are called Yarn A and Yarn B. Mix and match the colours for each block, so that no 6 blocks are the same.

- The turning chain 3 at the start of each round counts as 1 treble stitch.

- For each half-square triangle, when changing colour from Yarn B to Yarn A on Round 2, on the first tr into the corner in Yarn A: yarn over in Yarn A, yarn under and hook up the small piece of Yarn A between Rounds 1 and 2 so that it forms an extra loop on the hook, and complete the stitch as normal, working the extra loop at the same time as the final loop of the hook. This will help hide the yarn carried and enclose it in the treble.

PATTERN

Make 6 Eight-Point Star Blocks. Each Eight-Point Star Block is made from 16 squares in 6 different colour combinations as follows:

Block 1 Yarn A Lilac Powder Yarn B Bronzed Olive
Block 2 Yarn A Ivory White Yarn B Eucalyptus Green
Block 3 Yarn A Eucalyptus Green Yarn B Hot Punk Pink
Block 4 Yarn A Cameo Rose Yarn B Lilac Powder
Block 5 Yarn A Bronzed Olive Yarn B Ivory White
Block 6 Yarn A Hot Punk Pink Yarn B Cameo Rose

Solid Square

Per block, make 4 solid squares in Yarn A, 4 solid squares in Yarn B.

F ch4, ss into 1st ch to form a ring. (4sts)
Rnd 1 ch3, 2tr into ring, *ch2 (corner), 3tr into ring; rep from * 2 more times, ch2, ss into top of ch3 to join, turn. (20sts)
Rnd 2 ss into corner, ch3, 1tr into corner, *3tr, (2tr, ch2, 2tr) into corner; rep from * 2 more times, 3tr, 2tr into corner, ch2, ss into top of ch3 to join. (36sts)
Cut and fasten off yarn with a ss. Weave in ends.

Half-Square triangle

Per block, make 8 half-square triangles in Yarn A and Yarn B.

F In Yarn A, ch4, ss into 1st ch to form a ring.
Rnd 1 ch3, 2tr into ring, ch2 (corner), 3tr into ring, change to Yarn B on last tr, ch2 (corner), 3tr into ring,

CHAPTER THREE: PATCHWORK SCARF

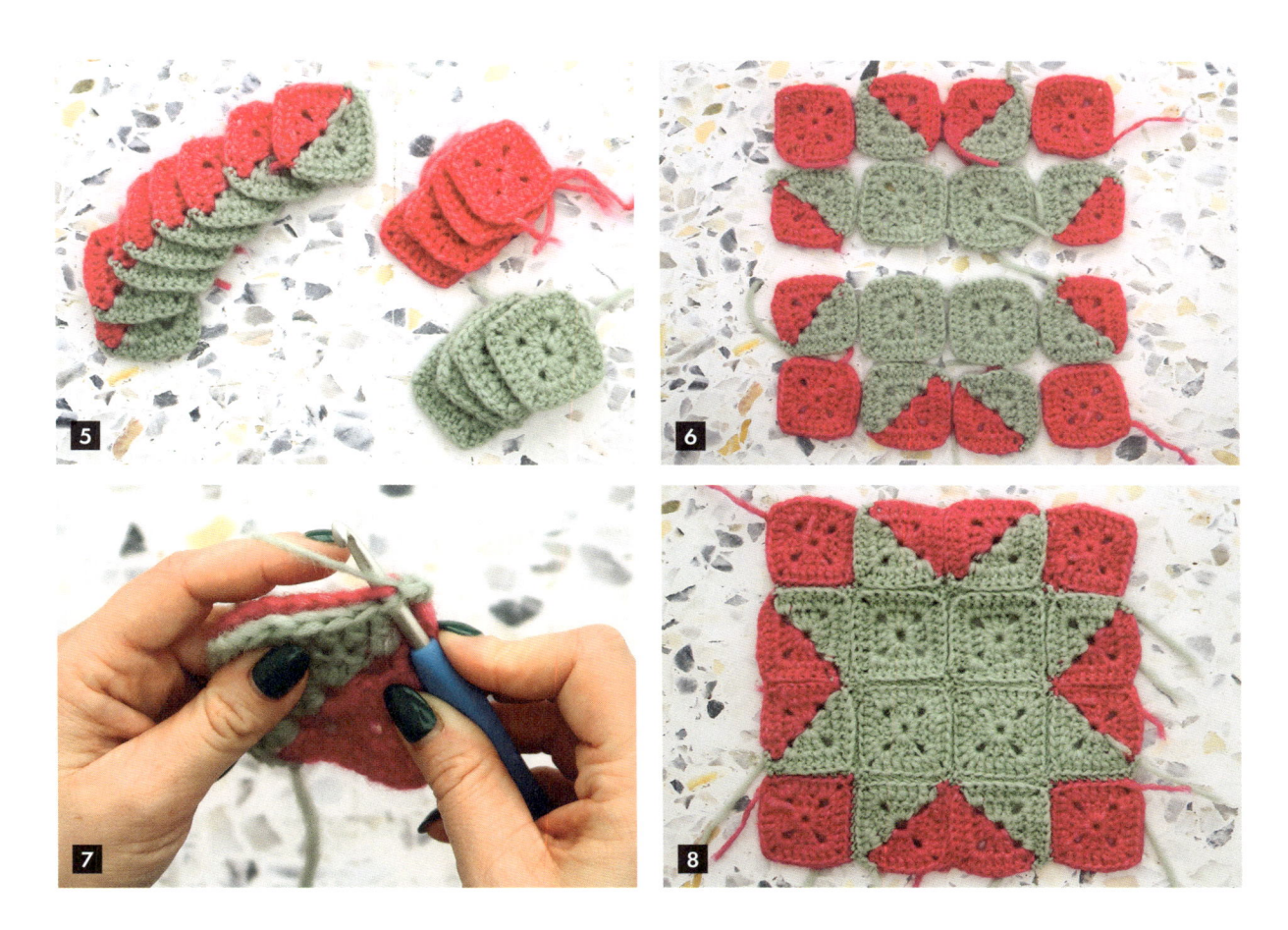

ch2 (corner), 3tr into ring, ch2, ss into top of ch3 to join, turn. (20sts) **(Fig. 1 & 2)**

Rnd 2 ss into corner, ch3, 1tr into corner, 3tr, (2tr, ch2, 2tr) into corner, 3tr, 2tr into corner, change to Yarn A on last tr – see tips, ch2, 2tr into corner, 3tr, (2tr, ch2, 2tr) into corner, 3tr, 2tr into corner, ch2, ss into top of ch3 to join. (36sts) **(Fig. 3 & 4)**

Cut and fasten off yarn with a ss. Weave in ends. **(Fig. 5)**

MAKING UP

When all 16 squares are made, join together in the star formation as shown. **(Fig. 6)**

To join, place the squares right sides together, join using a double crochet stitch through the back loops only of the square in front and of the square behind. **(Fig. 7)**

When joining your squares, use the Yarn A, or the main star colour, to join the edges, except when joining 2 squares where Yarn B meets Yarn B. Use Yarn B to join these squares to make for a more harmonious join on the reverse.

Join each block in the following order: Top and second row; third and bottom row; second and third row; first and second column, second and third column, third and fourth column. **(Fig. 8)**

When all 6 blocks are made, join them together in one long strip using the same joining method. Weave in all ends and place the join on the reverse.

chapter four: winter

This chapter's makes are all about cosying up and hunkering down. From the geometric hat to the leopard-print cowl, yarns are chunky, patterns are detailed and colours are soft and warm. Warm up your floors too, with a chunky scrap-yarn rug. Before you get busy making gifts for others though, make sure you hook up a luxe stocking for yourself - they'll make every Christmas extra special.

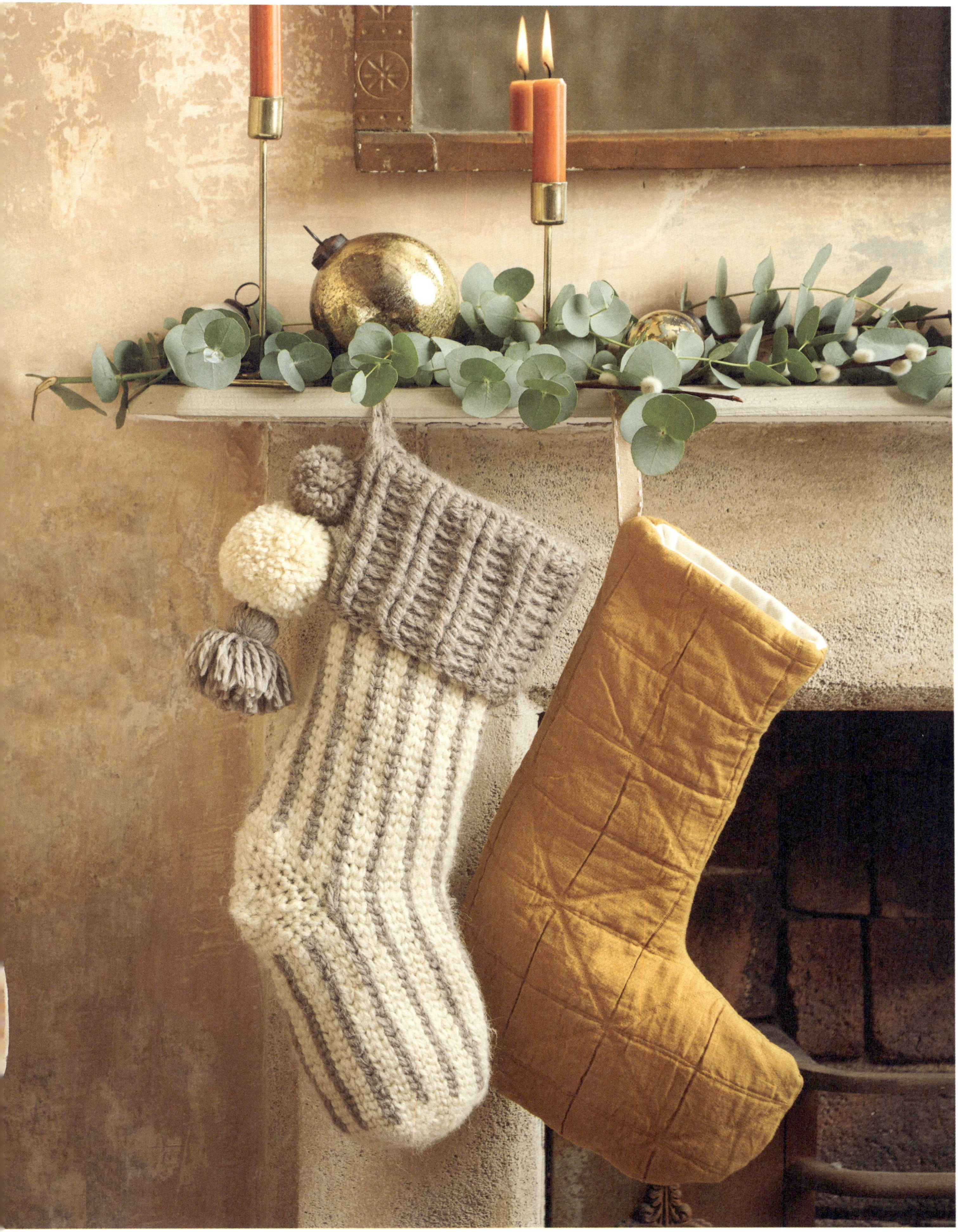

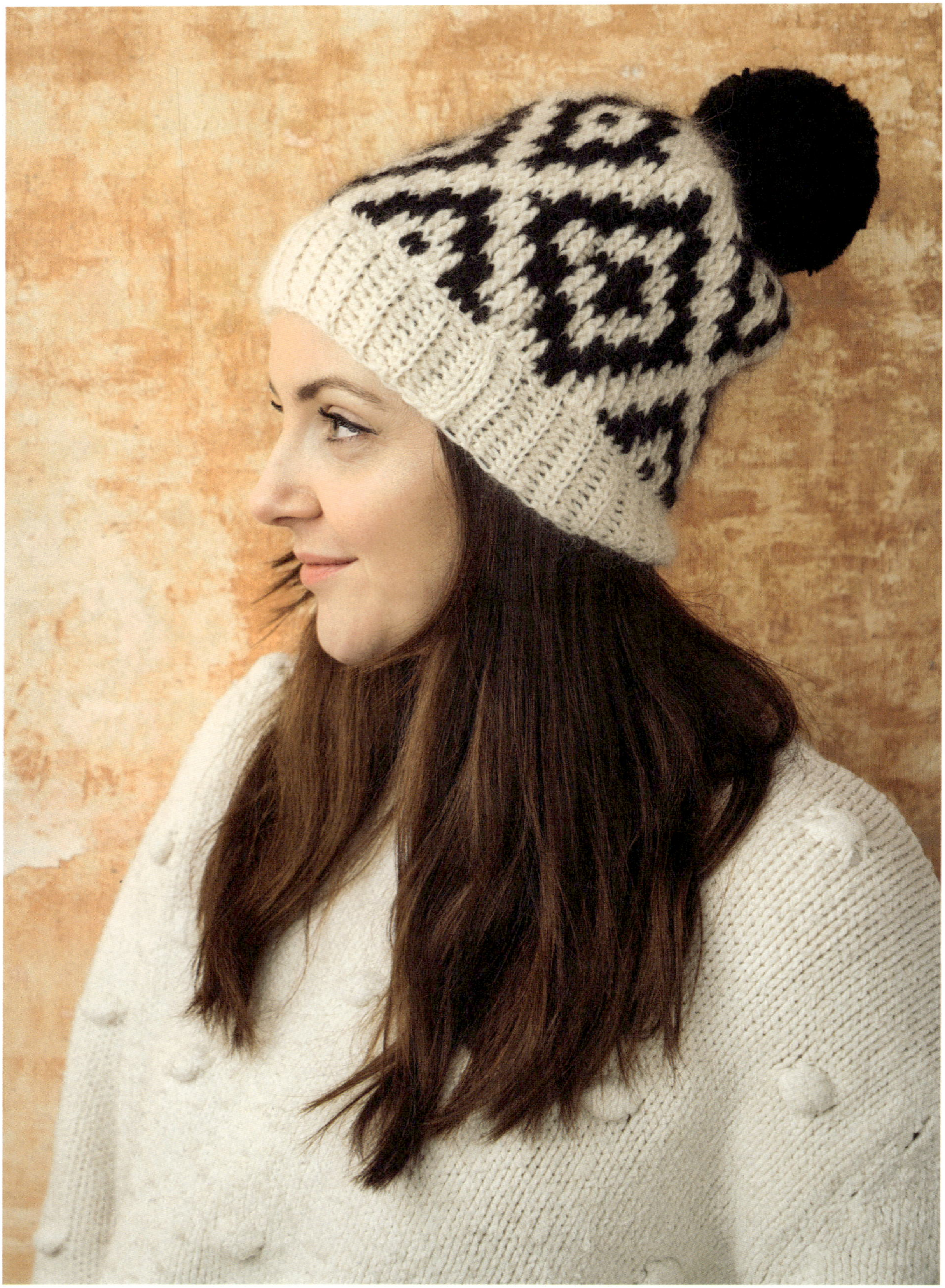

geo hat

I love crochet colourwork, but the off-set nature of crochet stitches can mean the colourwork isn't as satisfying as in knitted designs. The front post stitches in this pattern keep the colours ultra crisp, whilst also creating a plush fabric. If you prefer a more subtle look, use tonal colours like white and cream, or pink and red.

You will need
- Rowan Kid Classic, 50g/140m/153yd, 70% Wool/22% Mohair/8% Polyamide, Aran weight
  Yarn A Feather (828) x 2 balls
  Yarn B Iron (892) x 1 ball
- 5mm crochet hook
- 4 stitch markers
- 8.5cm pom pom maker

Yarn profile
Soft and warm, this wool blend yarn makes for a super cosy hat in striking colours.

Finished size
H22cm x C53cm

Techniques – see p.12
Back Loop Only
Crochet Colourwork
Fair Isle Crochet
Post Stitches
Working in the Round – Join Method

Gauge
10cm x 10cm = 18sts x 15 rounds when worked in FPtr pattern

LINDSEY'S TIPS

- The brim is worked flat, then joined, after which the body of the hat is worked in the round, joining at the end of each round.

- To create a more invisible seam, when joining at the end of each round, join to the top of the first front post treble stitch from the previous round, rather than the top of the starting chain.

- Written instructions are provided overleaf, but you may find it easier to follow the chart once you get going.

MODERN CROCHET STYLE

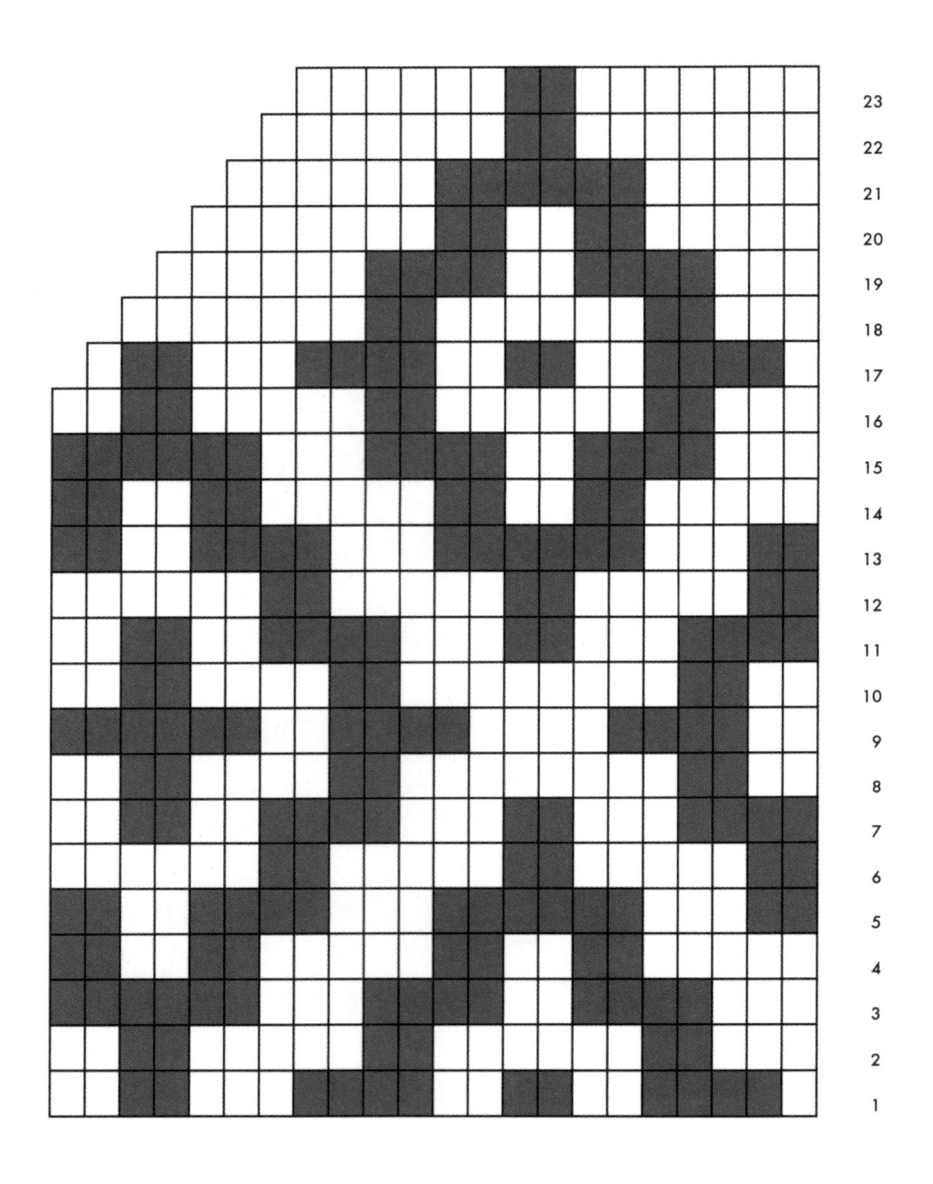

KEY

Yarn A ☐
Yarn B ■

CHART

The chart for this piece is read from right to left on every row. It covers Rounds 1-23 and shows just one repeat, with this section being repeated 4 times around the hat. Use the four stitch markers to mark the start or end of each pattern repeat, to help keep your place and work the pattern. Each square on the chart represents a front post treble stitch.

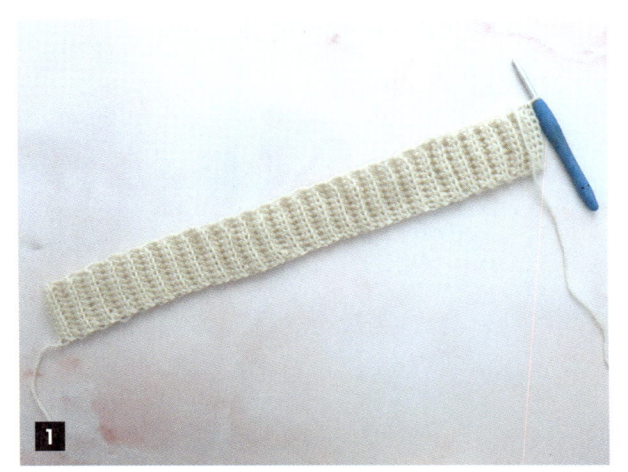

CHAPTER FOUR: GEO HAT

1

2

3

PATTERN
Work the brim
In Yarn A

F ch11.

Row 1 starting in 3rd ch from hook, 9htr in BLO, turn. (10sts)

Row 2 ch2 (counts as a st), 9htr in BLO, turn.

Rows 3-59, or until piece measures 50cm, Rep row 2. **(Fig. 1)**

Row 60 ch1, bring both ends of the long thin piece round to meet each other, and crochet together by working 10dc in BLO through both layers of the piece, joining the F chain to row 59. **(Fig. 2)**

Rotate the piece 90 degrees without turning, and evenly work 88dc around the brim of the hat. Use 4 stitch markers to help mark out the hat into quarters, placing them every 22sts, ss into top of 1st dc to join. (88sts) **(Fig. 3)**

Work the hat
Bring in Yarn B and carry behind the work in floats when not in use, fair isle style.

Rnd 1 ch2A (does not count as a stitch throughout body section), *1FPtrA, 4FPtrB, 2FPtrA, 2FPtrB, 2FPtrA, 4FPtrB, 3FPtrA, 2FPtrB, 2FPtrA; rep from * 3 more times, ss into top of 1st FPtr of the rnd (not the

87

ch2) to join. (88sts) **(Fig. 4 & 5)**

Rnd 2 ch2A, *3FPtrA, 2FPtrB, 6FPtrA, 2FPtrB, 5FPtrA, 2FPtrB, 2FPtrA; rep from * 3 more times, ss into top of 1st FPtr of the rnd to join.

Rnd 3 ch3A, *3FPtrA, 4FPtrB, 2FPtrA, 4FPtrB, 3FPtrA, 6FPtrB; rep from * 3 more times, ss into top of 1st FPtr of the rnd to join.

Rnd 4 ch2A, *5FPtrA, 2FPtrB, 2FPtrA, 2FPtrB, 5FPtrA, 2FPtrB, 2FPtrA, 2FPtrB; rep from * 3 more times, ss into top of 1st FPtr of the rnd to join.

Rnd 5 ch2B, *2FPtrB, 3FPtrA, 6FPtrB, 3FPtrA, 4FPtrB, 2FPtrA, 2FPtrB; rep from * 3 more times, ss into top of 1st FPtr of the rnd to join.

Rnd 6 ch2B, *2FPtrB, 5FPtrA, 2FPtrB, 5FPtrA, 2FPtrB, 6FPtrA; rep from * 3 more times, ss into top of 1st FPtr of the rnd to join.

Rnd 7 ch2B, *4FPtrB, 3FPtrA, 2FPtrB, 3FPtrA, 4FPtrB, 2FPtrA, 2FPtrB, 2FPtrA; rep from * 3 more times, ss into top of 1st FPtr of the rnd to join.

Rnd 8 ch2A, *2FPtrA, 2FPtrB, 8FPtrA, 2FPtrB, 4FPtrA, 2FPtrB, 2FPtrA; rep from * 3 more times, ss into top of 1st FPtr of the rnd to join.

Rnd 9 ch2A, *2FPtrA, 4FPtrB, 4FPtrA, 4FPtrB, 2FPtrA, 6FPtrB; rep from * 3 more times, ss into top of 1st FPtr of the rnd to join.

Rnd 10 rep Rnd 8.
Rnd 11 rep Rnd 7.
Rnd 12 rep Rnd 6.
Rnd 13 rep Rnd 5.
Rnd 14 rep Rnd 4.
Rnd 15 rep Rnd 3.
Rnd 16 rep Rnd 2. **(Fig. 6)**
Rnd 17 ch2A, *1FPtrA, 4FPtrB, 2FPtrB, 2FPtrA, 4FPtrB, 3FPtrA, 2FPtrB, FPtr2togA; rep from * 3 more

times, ss into top of 1st FPtr of the rnd to join. (84sts)
Rnd 18 ch2A, *3FPtrA, 2FPtrB, 6FPtrA, 2FPtrB, 6FPtrA, FPtr2togA; rep from * 3 more times, ss into top of 1st FPtr of the rnd to join. (80sts)
Rnd 19 ch2A, *3FPtrA, 4FPtrB, 2FPtrA, 4FPtrB, 5FPtrA, FPtr2togA; rep from * 3 more times, ss into top of 1st FPtr of the rnd to join. (76sts)
Rnd 20 ch2A, *5FPtrA, 2FPtrB, 2FPtrA, 2FPtrB, 6FPtrA, FPtr2tog; rep from * 3 more times, ss into top of 1st FPtr of the rnd to join. (72sts)
Rnd 21 ch2A, *5FPtrA, 6FPtrB, 5FPtrA, FPtr2togA; rep from * 3 more times, ss into top of 1st FPtr of the rnd to join. (68sts)
Rnd 22 ch2A, *7FPtrA, 2FPtrB, 6FPtrA, FPtr2togA; rep from * 3 more times, ss into top of 1st FPtr of the rnd to join. (64sts)
Rnd 23 ch2A, *7FPtrA, 2FPtrB, 5FPtrA, FPtr2togA; rep from * 3 more times, ss into top of 1st FPtr of the rnd to join. (60sts)
Cut Yarn B and secure by weaving in end.
Rnd 24 ch2A, 30FPtr2togA, ss into top of 1st FPtr of the rnd to join. (30sts) **(Fig. 7)**
Rnd 25 ch2A, 15FPtr2togA, ss into top of 1st FPtr of the rnd to join. (15sts)
Cut Yarn A leaving a 15cm long tail. Thread the tail onto a yarn needle, and weave in and out of the top of the stitches of Rnd 25. Pull to close hole and weave in ends to secure. **(Fig. 8)**

MAKING UP
Using the remainder of Yarn B and a 8.5cm or larger pom pom maker, create a pom pom to finish off your hat. Sew into the top of your hat through the centre of Rnd 25, and weave in end to fasten off. **(Fig. 9)**

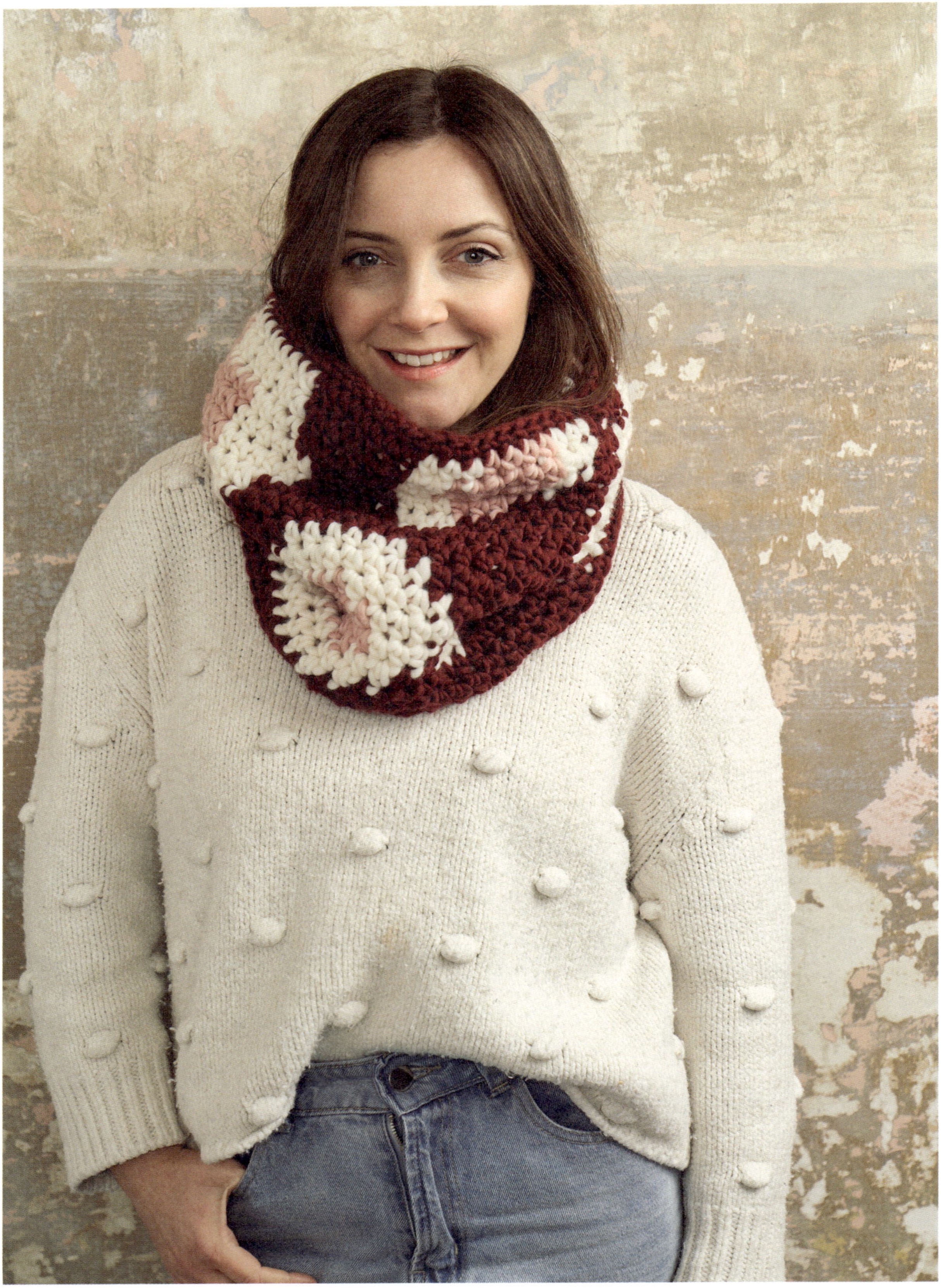

leopard cowl

Introducing... the oversized leopard cowl. Did you think I'd go the whole book without including a leopard-print project?! The pattern is large, so from some angles it's not totally obvious it's leopard print, which I like for it's subtlety.

You will need
- Stitch and Story The Chunky Wool, 100g/65m/71yd, 100% Merino Wool, chunky weight
  Yarn A Sangria Red x 2 balls
  Yarn B Ivory White x 1 ball
  Yarn C Dust Pink x 1 ball
- 10mm crochet hook

Yarn profile
This Merino wool is deliciously chunky and squishy. A neutral version of this cowl in white, cream and brown would also work wonderfully.

Finished size
H30cm x W40cm

Techniques – see p.12
Crochet Colourwork
Fair Isle Crochet
Working in the Round – Join Method

Gauge
10cm x 10cm = 8sts x 6 rounds, worked in dc pattern.

LINDSEY'S TIPS

- The cowl is worked in rounds, joining at the end of each round. Do not turn.
- Starting chains do not count as stitches.
- Where the pattern reads 7htrB – this should be read as 7 half treble crochet in Yarn B, and so on.
- The colourwork used is similar to that in Fair Isle knitting, where the unused yarns are carried behind the work in floats. Approx. every 4th stitch, work over the top of the other colours, to catch the floats and prevent them from getting too long.
- Written instructions are provided below, but you may find it easier to follow the chart once you get going.

MODERN CROCHET STYLE

KEY

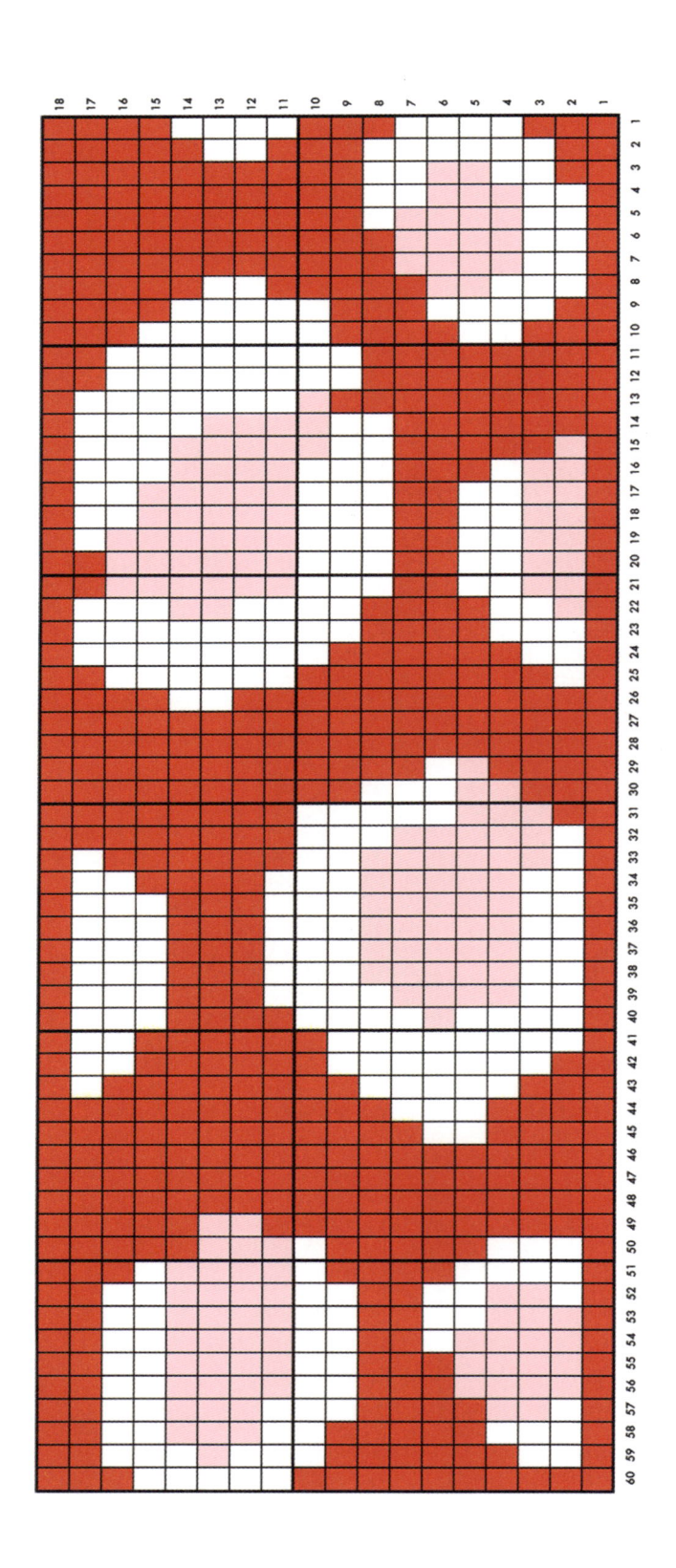

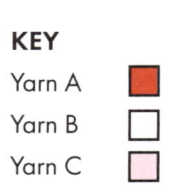

Yarn A ■

Yarn B ☐

Yarn C ▢

CHART

Read the chart from right to left for each round, starting bottom right and working upwards.
Use the chart or the row-by-row instructions below to work the colour work pattern for the cowl.
Each square on the chart represents a htr stitch.

CHAPTER FOUR: LEOPARD COWL

1

2

3

4

PATTERN

F In Yarn A, ch60. Bring the chain round to create a circle, without twisting, ss into the first chain to join. (60sts) **(Fig. 1)**

Rnd 1 ch2A, 60htrA, ss to top of 1st htr to join. (60sts)
Bring in Yarns B and C and carry behind the work as floats until needed, catching floats every 4th stitch by crocheting a stitch over the top of both floats.
(Fig. 2 & 3)

Rnd 2 ch2A, 3htrA, 5htrB, 6htrA, 8htrC, 3htrB, 6htrA, 10htrB, 8htrA, 3htrB, 4htrC, 3htrB, 1htrA, ss to top of 1st htr to join. **(Fig. 4)**

Rnd 3 ch2A, 1htrA, 8htrB, 6htrA, 6htrC, 3htrB, 6htrA, 3htrC, 9htrB, 7htrA, 2htrB, 6htrC, 2htrB, 1htrA and colour change to B, ss to top of 1st htr to join.
Rnd 4 ch2B, 3htrB, 4htrC, 3htrB, 5htrA, 8htrB, 6htrA, 10htrC, 4htrB, 6htrA, 2htrB, 6htrC, 1htrB, 2htrA and colour change to B, ss to top of 1st htr to join.
Rnd 5 ch2B, 2htrB, 6htrC, 2htrB, 6htrA, 5htrB, 7htrA, 11htrC, 6htrB, 5htrA, 3htrB, 3htrC, 4htrA and colour change to B, ss to top of 1st htr to join.
Rnd 6 ch2B, 2htrB, 6htrC, 1htrB, 19htrA, 3htrB, 9htrC, 5htrA, 6htrA, 3htrB, 6htrA and colour change to B, ss to top of 1st htr to join.
Rnd 7 ch2B, 4htrB, 3htrC, 22htrA, 2htrB, 8htrC,

93

MODERN CROCHET STYLE

5

6

7

5htrB, 16htrA, ss to top of 1st htr to join.
Rnd 8 ch2A, 1htrA, 4htrB, 8htrA, 8htrB, 8htrA, 3htrB, 6htrC, 5htrB, 17htrA, ss to top of 1st htr to join.
Rnd 9 ch2A, 10htrA, 2htrB, 1htrA, 10htrB, 7htrA, 12htrB, 9htrA, 6htrB, 3htrA, ss to top of 1st htr to join.
Rnd 10 ch2A, 8htrA, 4htrB, 3htrC, 9htrB, 6htrA, 10htrB, 9htrA, 10htrB, 1htrA and colour change to B, ss to top of 1st htr to join. **(Fig. 5)**
(Fig. 6 shows inside)
Rnd 11 ch2B, 1htrB, 7htrA, 5htrB, 8htrC, 4htrB, 8htrA, 6htrB, 10htrA, 7htrC, 4htrB, ss to top of 1st htr to join.
Rnd 12 ch2B, 2htrB, 5htrA, 6htrB, 8htrC, 4htrB, 23htrA, 10htrC, 2htrB, ss to top of 1st htr to join.
Rnd 13 ch2B, 2htrB, 5htrA, 6htrB, 9htrC, 4htrB, 22htrA, 11htrC, 1htrB, ss to top of 1st htr to join.
Rnd 14 ch2B, 1htrB, 7htrA, 6htrB, 8htrC, 4htrB, 24htrA, 8htrC, 2htrB and colour change to A, ss to top of 1st htr to join.
Rnd 15 ch2A, 9htrA, 7htrB, 5htrC, 4htrB, 9htrA, 6htrB, 10htrA, 10htrB and colour change to A, ss to top of 1st htr to join.
Rnd 16 ch2A, 10htrA, 8htrB, 3htrC, 4htrB, 8htrA, 9htrB, 9htrA, 8htrB, 1htrA, ss to top of 1st htr to join.
Rnd 17 ch2A, 12htrA, 7htrB, 2htrA, 3htrB, 8htrA, 11htrB, 17htrA, ss to top of 1st htr to join.
Cut and weave in Yarns B and C to secure them.
Rnd 18 ch2A, 60htrA, ss to top of 1st htr to join.
Cut Yarn A and fasten off with a ss, weave in ends.
(Fig. 7)

CHAPTER FOUR: LEOPARD COWL

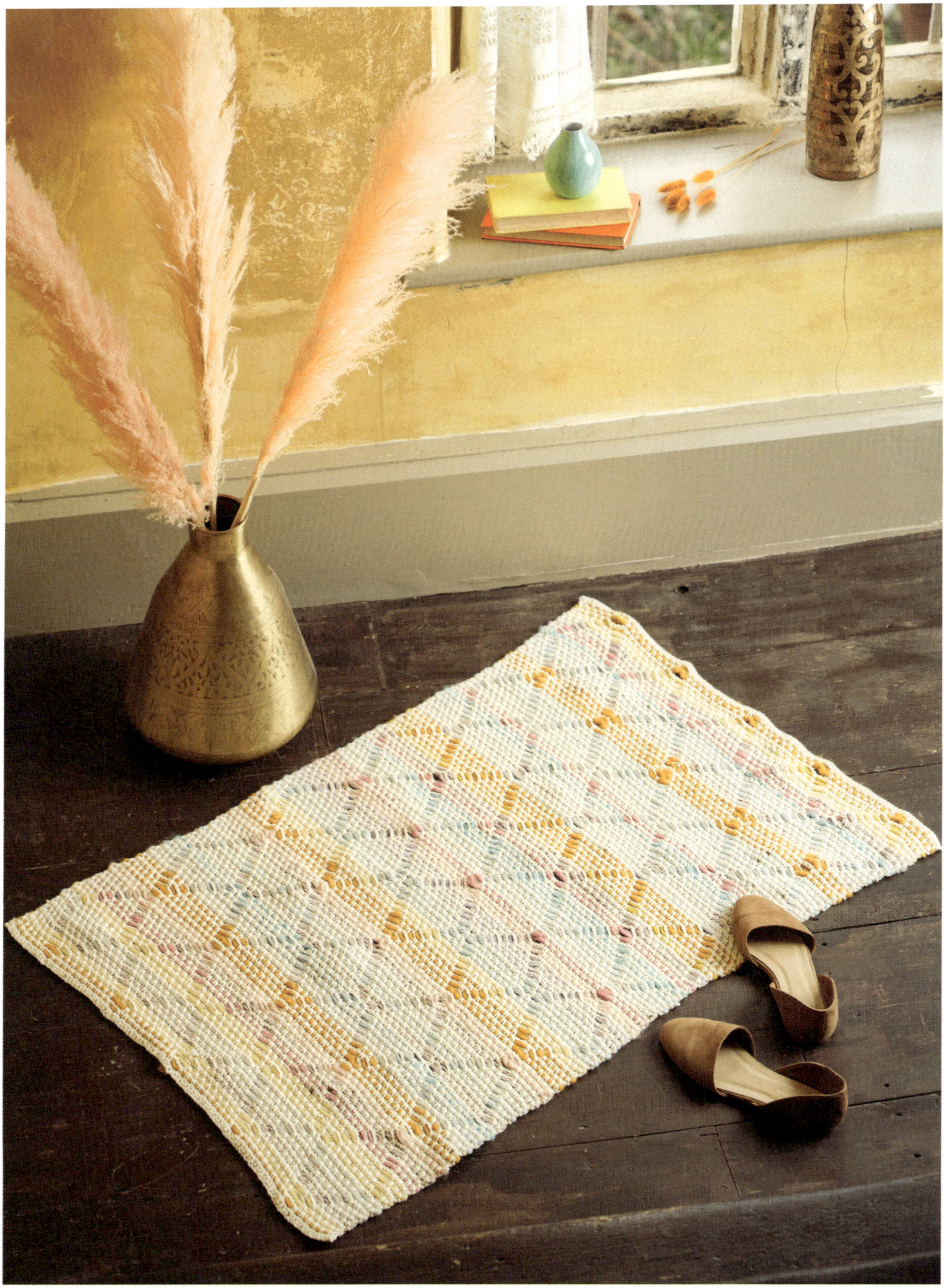

scrap rug

In the early stages of planning this book, I knew I wanted to include projects to help use up your scraps. Scrap projects can be messy or confusing; the secret to this project is to use one, unifying cotton yarn throughout. Cutting your scraps to similar lengths before you start also harmonises the project for maximum impact.

You will need
- Rico Design Creative Cotton Aran, 50g/85m/93yd per ball, 100% cotton
  Yarn A Cream (60) x 7 balls
  Yarn B 100 x 150cm lengths of chunky yarn, in colours of your choice. I used pinks, blues, mustard, yellow and lilac
- 5mm crochet hook

Yarn profile
Using an Aran-weight cotton gives strength and unity to the project. The more the colour contrast between the scrap and Aran yarn, the more obvious the pattern will be. If your scraps are all pale, use a darker Aran yarn. If you don't have scrap yarn, you can use a ball of yarn, or cut lengths from full balls of yarn.

Finished size
65cm x 100cm

Techniques – see p.12
Filet Crochet
Tapestry Crochet

Gauge
10cm x 10cm = 18sts x 11 rows, when worked in pattern (chain stitches count as stitches)

LINDSEY'S TIPS

- The turning chain does not count as a stitch throughout. All other chains in a row are to be counted as stitches and, when written in the pattern, indicate making a chain and missing the double crochet below.

- When working the filet pattern, all double crochets are made into chain spaces, except when working above a chain 3 or chain 5, where you should work into the chain stitch itself.

- Allow all knots to sit on the same side of the rug.

- When turning your rug, allow the yarn to sit on the same side each time. See Techniques, Tapestry Crochet p.12.

- The chunky yarn is passive in this pattern: it is never crocheted with but carried throughout, tapestry crochet style.

PATTERN
Scrap ball

Step 1 Cut 100 x 150cm lengths of chunky yarn. If you have DK or thin aran weight yarns, you could include them in your scrap ball held double, to mimic the weight of one strand of chunky yarn. Don't worry if your scrap yarns are different fibres or textures – it will add to the fun! **(Fig. 1)**

Step 2 Tie each of your 100 lengths of yarn together using a double knot, leaving a tail of at least 5cm on each knot. **(Fig. 2)**

Step 2 As you tie the lengths together, start to wind your scraps in a ball. Every now and again, tie two scraps the same colour together consecutively, to create a thicker block of colour in the finished rug. **(Fig. 3 & 4)**

CHAPTER FOUR: SCRAP RUG

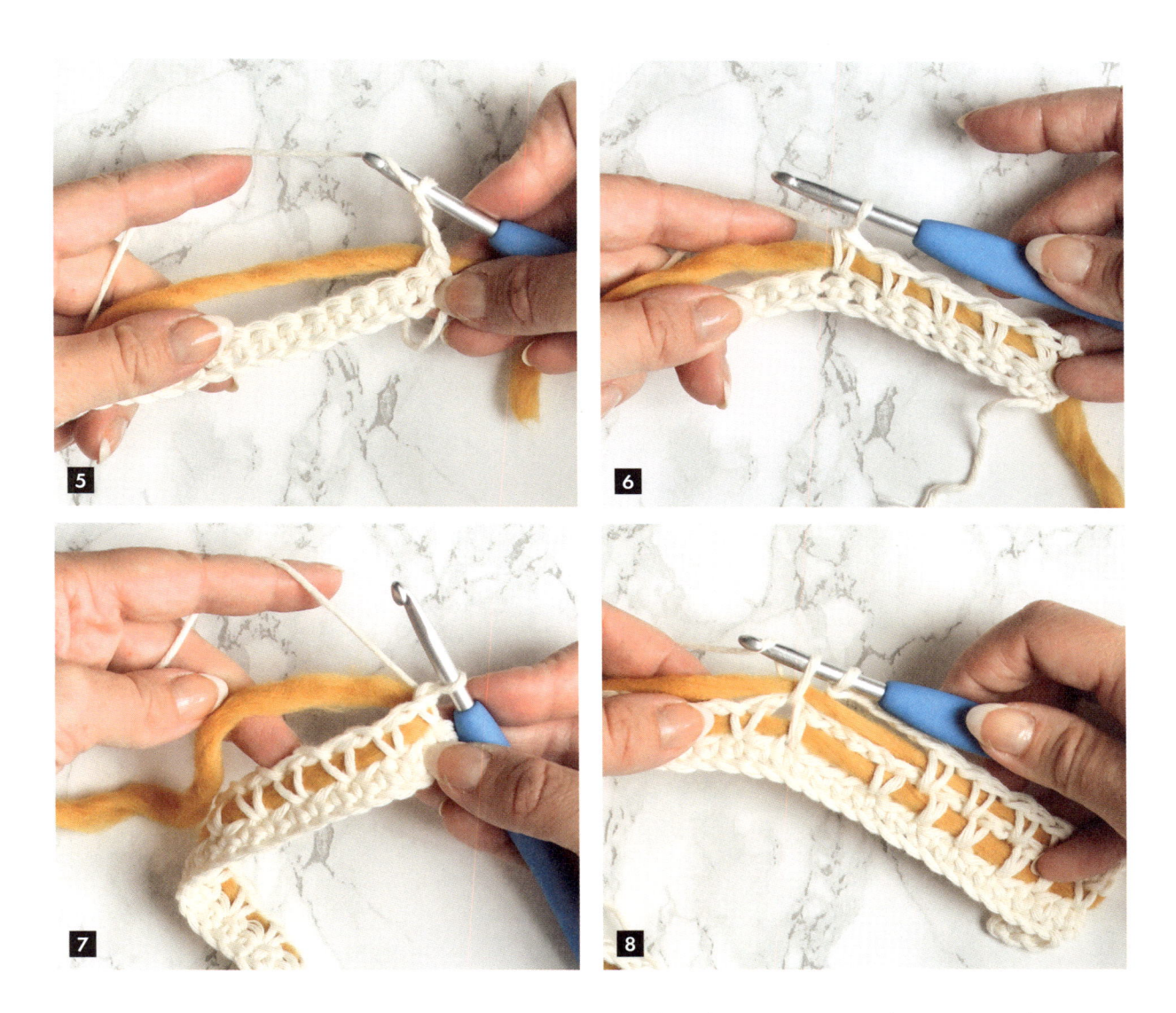

Rug

F Using Yarn A, loosely ch113.

Row 1 ch1 (does not count as a st here), work 1dc in each ch along, turn, and bring in Yarn B, holding it on top of row 1. (113sts) **(Fig. 5)**

Row 2 working over the Yarn B in this and all subsequent rows, ch1, dc, *(ch1, dc)x5, ch3, (dc, ch1)x4, dc; rep from * 4 more times, until 2sts remain, ch1, dc, turn. **(Fig. 6)**

Row 3 ch1, 2dc, *(ch1, dc)x4, ch5, (dc, ch1)x4, dc; rep from * 4 more times, until 1st remains, dc, turn. **(Fig. 7 & 8)**

Row 4 ch1, dc, *(ch1, dc)x4, ch3, dc, ch3, (dc, ch1x3, dc; rep from * 4 more times until 2sts remain, ch1, dc, turn. **(Fig. 9, overleaf)**

Row 5 ch1, 2dc, *(ch1, dc)x3, ch3, dc, ch1, dc, ch3, (dc, ch1)x3, dc; rep from * 4 more times until 1st remains, dc.

Row 6 ch1, dc, *(ch1, dc)x3, ch3, (dc, ch1)x2, dc, ch3, (dc, ch1)x2, dc; rep from * 4 more times until

99

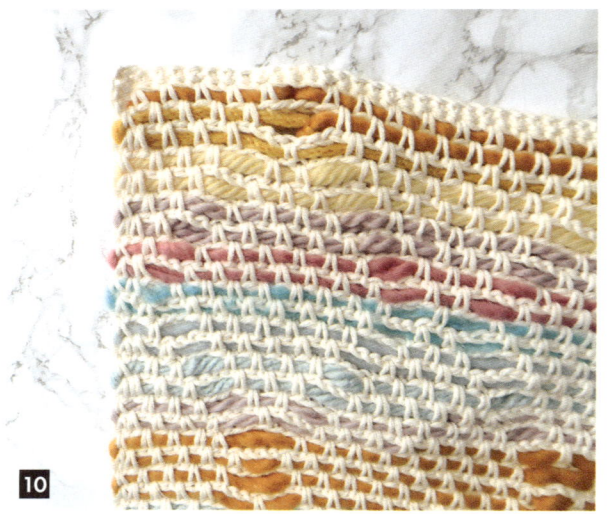

2sts remain, ch1, dc, turn.

Row 7 ch1, 2dc, *(ch1, dc)x2, ch3, (dc, ch1)x3, dc, ch3, (dc, ch1)x2, dc; rep from * 4 more times until 1st remains, dc, turn.

Row 8 ch1, dc, *(ch1, dc)x2, ch3, (dc, ch1)x4, dc, ch3, dc, ch1, dc; rep from * 4 more times until 2sts remain, ch1, dc, turn.

Row 9 ch1, 2dc, *ch1, dc, ch3, (dc, ch1)x5, dc, ch3, dc, ch1, dc; rep from * 4 more times until 1st remains, dc, turn.

Row 10 ch1, dc, *ch1, dc, ch3, (dc, ch1)x6, dc, ch3, dc; rep from * 4 more times until 2sts remain, ch1, dc, turn.

Row 11 ch1, 2dc, *ch3, (dc, ch1)x7, dc, ch3, dc; rep from * 4 more times until 1st remains, dc.

Row 12 rep Row 10.
Row 13 rep Row 9.
Row 14 rep Row 8.
Row 15 rep Row 7.
Row 16 rep Row 6.

CHAPTER FOUR: SCRAP RUG

12

Row 17 rep Row 5.
Row 18 rep Row 4.
Row 19 rep Row 3.
Rows 20-109 rep rows 2-19 5 more times.
Row 110 rep row 2. At end of row, cut Yarn B, leaving a long tail, turn.
Row 111 ch1, dc in each st along. Work into the ch-sts above ch3 sections, and into the ch-sps above ch1s. Cut Yarn A yarn and fasten off with a ss. Sew in ends for both yarns. **(Fig. 10 & 11)**

MAKING UP
Where each 150cm length of scrap yarn was tied together, you will have a small knot. These should all be sitting on the same side of the scrap rug. Either leave these showing as a feature (think visible mending!) and use this as the front of your rug, or sew them all in and keep this side as the reverse. **(Fig. 12)**

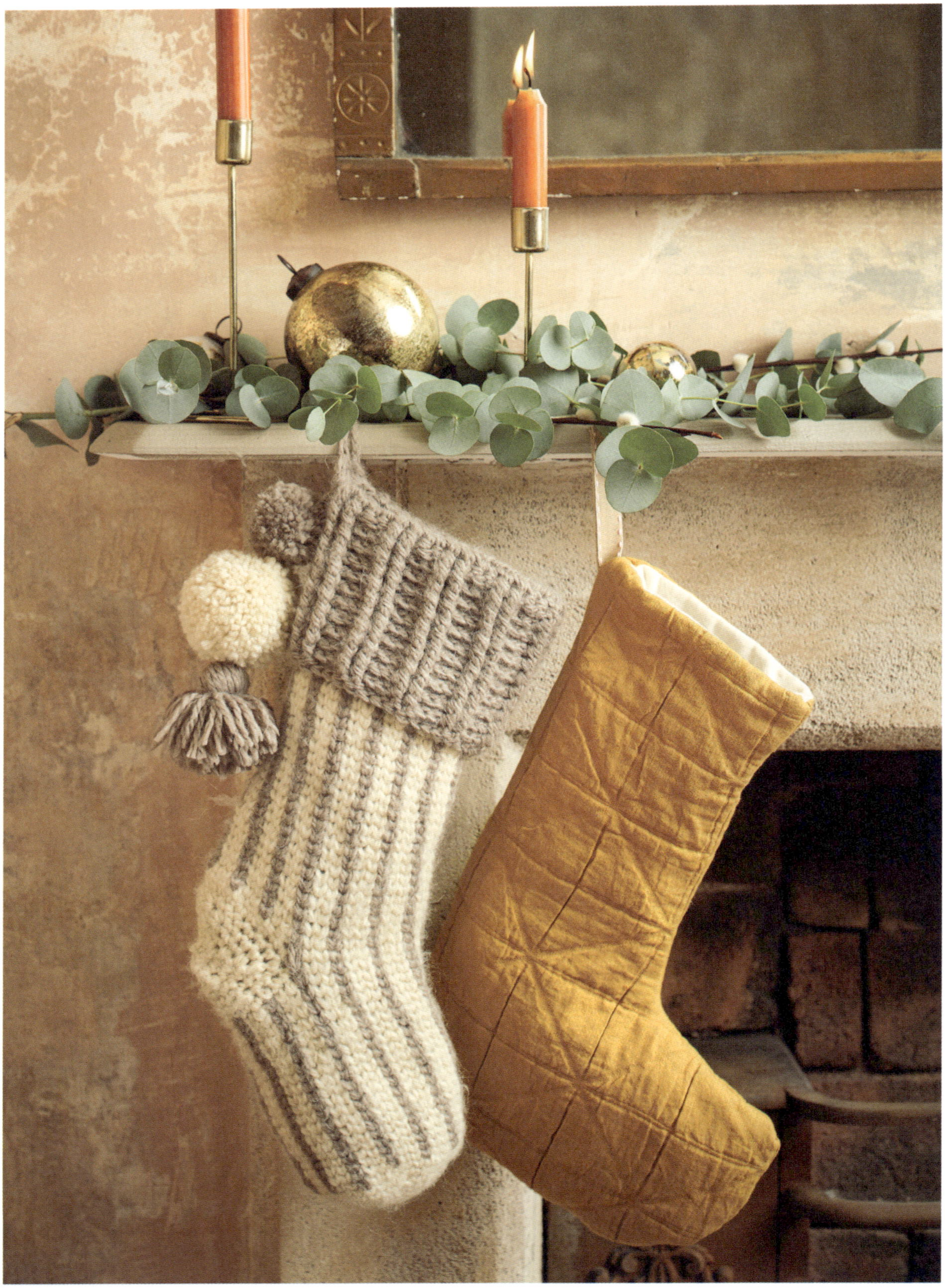

scandi stocking

I know Christmas is really about the kids... but don't we deserve a little treat for ourselves too? This grown-up stocking hits both sophisticated and cosy notes - which I love. The waistcoat stitch transforms your crochet to look like knitting, and also creates a really sturdy fabric, ideal for stuffing full of gifts.

You will need
- Knitcraft by Hobbycraft Leader of the Pac Aran yarn, 100g/170m/185yd, 90% Acrylic/10% Alpaca
  Yarn A Cream x 1 ball
  Yarn B Mink x 1 ball
- 6mm crochet hook
- Stitch marker

Yarn profile
This Aran-weight yarn is one of my favourites. It works up smoothly and quickly, and the 10% Alpaca makes all the difference.

Finished size
H45cm x W17cm

Techniques – see p.12
Crochet Colourwork
Fair Isle Crochet
Magic Loop
Post Stitches
Waistcoat Stitch
Working in the Round – Spiral Method

Gauge
10cm x 10cm = 13sts x 14 rounds when worked in waistcoat stitch with colour changes

LINDSEY'S TIPS

- Work your waistcoat stitches loosely, to make it easier to get your hook in the centre of the stitch on the next round.

- Because of the short colour changes in this pattern, the second colour is not carried inside the work but left in floats behind the work. When you colour change, try not to pull too tightly or the floats will distort the work.

- Use a stitch marker at the end of each round to help keep your place.

- Where the pattern reads 2wcB – this should be read as 2 waistcoat stitches in Yarn B, and so on.

PATTERN

Toe and leg

F Using Yarn A, create a ML and ch1.
Round 1 6dc into ML, pull closed. (6sts)
Round 2 *dcinc; rep from * 5 more times. (12sts)
Round 3 *dcinc, 1dc; rep from * 5 more times. (18sts)
Round 4 *dcinc, 2dc; rep from * 5 more times. (24sts)
Round 5 *dcinc, 3dc; rep from * 5 more times. (30sts)
Round 7 *dcinc, 4dc; rep from * 5 more times. (36sts)
Round 8 36dc.
Round 9 36wc.
Introduce Yarn B, and work colour changes between A and B for stitches as indicated.
Round 10 *2wcA, 1wcB; rep from * 11 more times.
Round 11-30 Rep Round 10. **(Fig. 1)**
Round 31 In Yarn A ch18, sk 15sts from Round 30, cut and fasten off Yarn B to prevent a long float, and reattach after ch section, *2wcA, 1wcB; rep from * 6 more times. (39sts) **(Fig. 2)**
Round 32 In Yarn A, 18dc into ch-sts from prev rnd, *2wcA, 1wcB; rep from * 6 more times. (39sts) **(Fig. 3)**
Round 33 *2wcA, 1wcB; rep from * 12 more times. **(Fig. 4)**
Rounds 34-52 Rep Round 33.
Round 53 *2wcA, 1wcB; rep from * 15 more times, until you reach edge of stocking, directly above the heel. **(Fig. 5)**

CHAPTER FOUR: SCANDI STOCKING

105

Cuff

Work remainder of stocking rounds in Yarn B.

Round 54 39dc.

Round 55 39htr.

Round 56-63 Rep Round 55. **(Fig. 6)**

Round 64 (ch10, ss into same htr as ch to form a loop), *2FPtr, 2BPtr; rep from * until 2sts remain, 2FPtr.

Round 65 Sk st with loop from prev round, *2FPtr, 2BPtr; rep from * until 2sts remain, 2FPtr. (38sts)

Round 66 *2FPtr, 2BPtr; rep from * until 2sts remain, 2FPtr.

Round 67-74 Rep Round 66. **(Fig. 7)**

Round 75 *2FPtr, 2BPtr; rep from * until 2sts remain, 1FPhtr, 1FPdc, 1ss.

Cut and fasten off yarn with a ss, weave in ends.

Fold the rib section of the stocking down at Round 64 so that it sits on the outside of the stocking, and the loop is visible on the edge.

(Fig. 8)

CHAPTER FOUR: SCANDI STOCKING

Heel
Using Yarn A, attach yarn to first skipped st from Round 30, work around skipped stitches and the underside of the ch from Round 31 in a circle. **(Fig. 9)**
Round 1 ch1, does not count as a st, 9dc, dc2tog, 9dc, dc2tog, 9dc, dc2tog. (30sts)
Round 2 *3dc, dc2tog; rep from * 5 more times. (24sts)
Round 3 *2dc, dc2tog; rep from * 5 more times. (18sts)
Round 4 *1dc, dc2tog; rep from * 5 more times. (12sts)
Round 5 *dc2tog; rep from * 5 more times. (6sts)
Cut and fasten off yarn with a ss, weave in and out of 6sts from heel round 5 to pull hole closed. Weave in ends.

MAKING UP
If you want to add an extra touch of luxe, create a pom pom tassel and attach to your stocking.

frequently asked questions

I'm a beginner, can I make the projects in this book?
Absolutely. I'm a big believer in learning as you go along. It's great to practise stitches and techniques if that's what interests you, but I'm personally so much more motivated to try a new technique or stitch if there's a project I want to try that uses them. My advice is to follow the photo tutorials and the pattern, and look up any new terms as you go along. You can find a beginner's section and FAQs on my website, www.lottieandalbert.co.uk. Google and YouTube are also your friend!

Do I need to do a gauge or tension swatch?
I am often asked this very good question. Gauge swatches are a little bit of a necessary evil. They are a little bit boring to make, but they will almost certainly save you time in the long run.
Because the designer of a pattern may have a different tension when crocheting to you, the hook and yarn they recommend may not give you the same finished size if your tension is different. This doesn't matter too much if it's a bag or a coaster, but if you are making a garment or a cushion, which need to fit precisely, it's definitely worth spending the extra ten minutes to make a test gauge swatch.
My top tip is to make the swatch with slightly more stitches and rows than the gauge guide specifies to give you a 10cm x 10cm square. This will help give you space to measure.

My gauge swatch is coming out much larger/smaller than the measurements given. What should I do?
Firstly, you haven't done anything wrong. Gauge or tension is personal to each crocheter and can vary enormously. Follow these instructions to find out what you can do to adjust your gauge and ensure your make comes out the right size.
If you have fewer stitches/rows in your 10cm x 10cm square than the number stated in the pattern that means your tension is looser than the designers, so try going down 0.5 or 1 hook size.
If you have more stitches/rows in your 10cm x 10cm square than the number stated in the pattern that means your tension is tighter than the designers, so try going up 0.5 or 1 hook size.

I'm left-handed, can I read the charts from left to right instead, as this makes more sense to me?
This depends slightly on the chart and the type of project. If the project is tapestry crochet and the fabric is reversible, it is absolutely fine to read the charts from left to right. All the patterns in this book are suitable for you to do this; you will just need to be mindful of your Wrong and Right sides in projects like the hat and cowl, which carry yarns on the reverse.

frequently asked questions

What are your favourite hooks to use?
This is such a personal thing, but my favourite are the Clover Amour ergonomic hooks with a soft handle. I find that metal and wooden hooks with no handle are a little hard on my hands. Hooks with handmade polymer clay handles look beautiful and look great for styling photo shoots, but because I hold my hook in a knife hold, I don't find them quite as comfortable.

Do you have any other tools you recommend?
The best thing about crochet is that it requires so few materials. A hook and yarn and you are good to go! The yarns included in this book are all from some of my favourite brands (see Page 110 for some stockist recommendations), so you can't go wrong if you start there.
To follow are a few other tools which I personally own and rate, which may also make your life easier.

Clover pom pom makers (the kind with two arms that fold in, and a pin connecting the middle) are my favourite pom pom makers. Get yours from
www.clover-mfg.com.

If you are trimming lots of pom poms, treat yourself to a really **sharp pair of scissors!** Fiskars have a great range.
www.fiskars.com.

Pony yarn needles, which have a flexible plastic loop instead of an eye, make sewing in ends so much faster.
Try *www.ponyneedles-europe.de.*

A square gauge swatch really speeds up measuring tension squares. Addi have a strong plastic kind with cut-out holes to check the mm size of hook/needles too *www.addineedles.co.uk.*
If you prefer a wooden ruler, Etsy has a great selection *www.etsy.com.*

Wooden blocking boards with pegs are helpful if you are blocking stacks of motifs or granny squares. However, my preferred method is to use pins into a foam board. The interlocking kind that are sold as floor puzzle pieces for kids are ideal, because you can use several together for larger pieces. Try Amazon or a local toy store.

Stainless steel pins are a must for blocking your makes without rusting! If you want to upgrade to a speciality set, KnitPro do some great Knit Blockers.
http://www.knitpro.eu.

If you have any other questions then message me on Instagram **@lottieandalbert** and I will reply to you there.

suppliers

With thanks to the following companies who supplied yarn for this book:

Hobbycraft
www.hobbycraft.co.uk
Return of the Mac p.72
Leader of the Pac p.102
Rico Design Creative Cotton Aran p.96

In Stitches
www.instichesstroud.co.uk
Adriafil Knitcol p.56

Rico Design
www.rico-design.de
Ricorumi DK p.46 & 60
Fashion Alpaca Dream p.50
Fashion Light Luxury p.50

Rowan
www.knitrowan.com
Kid Classic p.84

Stitch and Story
www.stitchandstory.com
The Chunky Wool p.90

Wool and the Gang
www.woolandthegang.com
Ra-Ra Raffia Yarn p.28
Buddy Hemp Yarn p.40
Shiny Happy Cotton p.46
Mixtape Yarn p.66
Feeling Good Yarn p.78

Woolly Mahoosive
www.woollymahoosive.com
5mm Macrame and Crochet Cord p.56
10mm chunky Macrame Cord p.60
www.makeeshop.com

Thanks also to:
Becki Clark
www.beckiclark.com
For creating the brush-lettering script for the Slogan Bath Mat p.66

Emily Ashbourn
www.makeeshop.com
For the leopard-print crochet hook used on the cover

Lucy Davidson
www.peasandneedles.co.uk
For creating the gorgeous linen stocking p.102

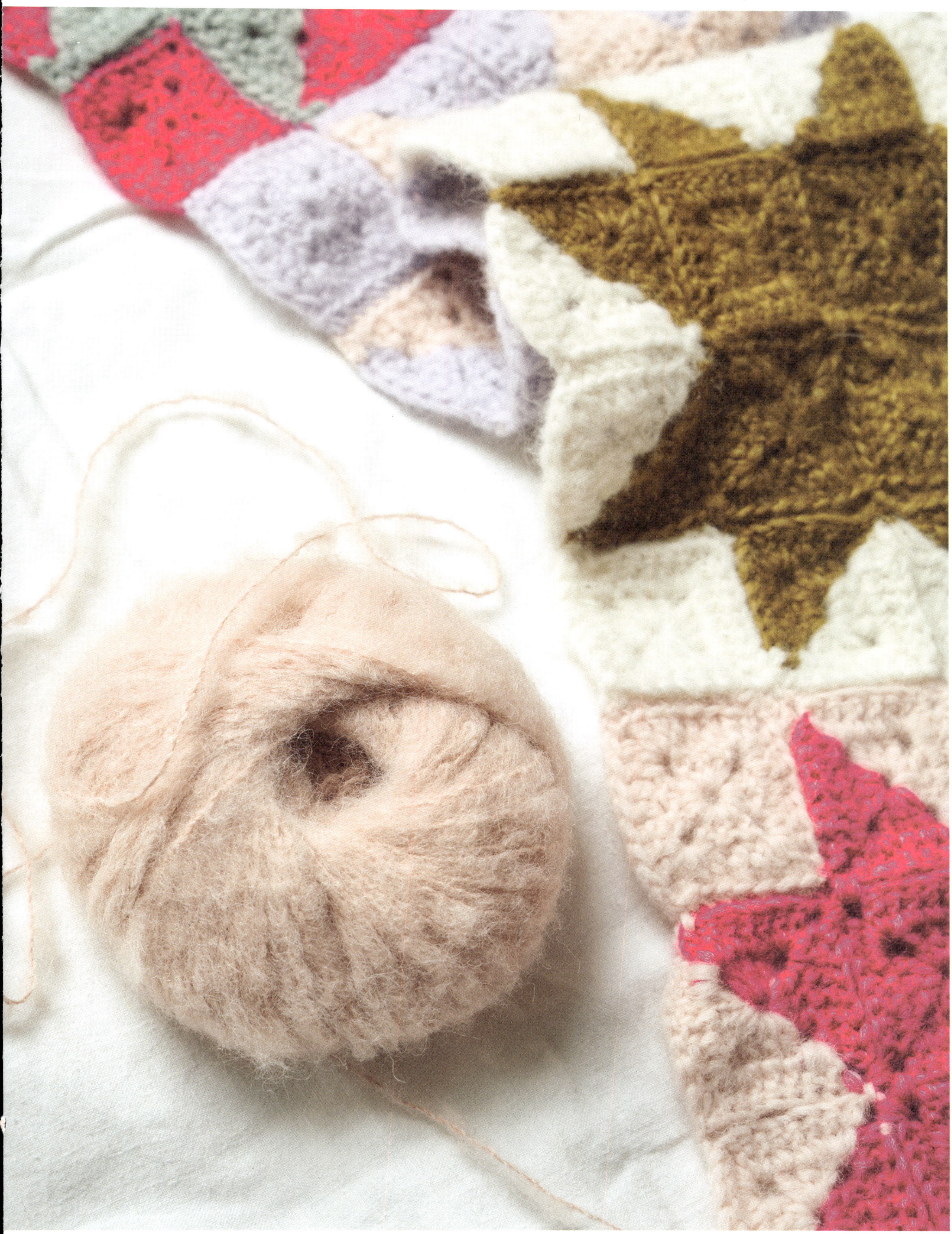

about the author

Lindsey is the face behind Lottie and Albert *www.lottieandalbert.co.uk*. A designer of popular modern crochet patterns, Lindsey shares her tutorials and makes on Instagram and YouTube to over 40,000 followers.

Alongside designing her own patterns, Lindsey has worked in publishing for over 10 years, most notably as the commissioning editor for creative crafts magazine, Mollie Makes. Lindsey has appeared as a guest judge on Kirstie Allsopp's Handmade Christmas TV show in the UK. She also runs a monthly crochet subscription box, Curate Crochet Box.

She lives in the Cotswolds with 1 husband, 3 children and an uncountable number of balls of yarn.

www.lottieandalbert.co.uk
www.curatecrochetbox.co.uk
www.instagram.com/lottieandalbert

Acknowledgements Huge thanks to Valerie Bracegirdle for her help as technical editor, Jesse Wild, who photographed my finished projects, Jaine Bevan for her wonderful styling, and Katherine Raderecht for commissioning me.